MEGA
DEAL
SECRETS

MEGA DEAL SECRETS

How to Find and Close the Biggest Deal of Your Career

JAMAL REIMER

WITH ANDY EARLE

SUMMITEER
PRESS

SUMMITEER
PRESS

Little Rock, Arkansas

Copyright © 2021 by JDSN Holdings LLC

Hardcover ISBN 978-1737765509 | Paperback ISBN 978-1737765523

eBook ISBN 978-1737765516

Library of Congress Control Number: 2021918118

Book production by The Pub Pros, Inc., www.thepubpros.com

Cover design by Zeljka Kojic

Interior illustrations by Lorna Nakell

Printed and bound in the United States of America

To that Unknowable Essence that some call God,
Whose servant I strive to be.

To Didar, Silas, and Nuria,
my family who make life worth living.

To my parents, Kathy and Dan,
who pointed me in the right direction.

TABLE OF CONTENTS

THE IMPOSSIBLE DEAL

A Mega Deal is a business transaction with the potential to change the fortunes of a company and impact the lives of many people. It's the kind of deal Robert Iger had in mind when he stepped into the conference room for his first board meeting as CEO of the Walt Disney Company in September 2005. The company was in a tailspin after fending off a hostile takeover attempt from Comcast, removing long-time CEO Michael Eisner from his post by force, and receiving harsh public criticism from Roy Disney, who referred to the selection process that put Iger into the executive role as a "sham."

It was a cool California evening, and anticipation hung in the air as Iger took his place for the first time at the head of the long conference table and faced down the ten men and women who made up Disney's board of directors—a few of whom had opposed his appointment to the bitter end.

Generally, a CEO's first board meeting isn't the time to propose a radical and risky new deal. In this situation Iger was supposed to give a rah-rah-go-get-'em motivational speech, show some financial projection graphs with lines trending sharply upward in the near future, and finish off with a bit of we're-all-in-this-together corporate talk. Then he was supposed to end the meeting early and spend the rest of the evening shaking hands, smiling, exchanging pleasantries, and trying to inspire confidence that he had everything under control.

Except Bob Iger had something very different in mind.

"As you all know," he said, jumping right into it, "Disney Animation is a real mess." He described a scene he'd witnessed a few weeks earlier, when he'd flown to China for the opening of Hong Kong Disneyland. As part of the opening ceremonies, the park put on a massive parade, and Iger watched as a long series of floats marched down Main Street. First came characters from all of Disney's most iconic films, like *Snow White and the Seven Dwarfs*, *Cinderella*, and *Peter Pan*. Then there were some big characters from Disney's hits of the 1980s and early '90s, like *The Little Mermaid*, *Beauty and the Beast*, *Aladdin*, and *The Lion King*. Finally, there were more recent characters from the films they had done with Pixar: *Toy Story*, *Finding Nemo*, and *Monsters, Inc.*

"Do you guys notice anything about this parade?" Bob asked the board members. They shook their heads. Nothing stood out to them about the floats. "There are barely any Disney characters from the last ten years," Iger concluded.

By pointing out this detail, Bob must have quietly set off silent explosions in the heads of all the board members. There was instant recognition of a massive problem. And a sense of dread and threat that can make the most powerful businesspeople squirm in their seats. Thoughts like *How could we have missed that?* were likely zipping around their neural networks, kicking off hits of adrenaline, preparing fight-or-flight responses.

This was a masterful display of revealing an insight, a major theme of this book and a skill every seller intent on closing Mega Deals needs in her toolbox.

He then displayed a list of recent Disney films: *The Hunchback of Notre Dame, Hercules, Mulan, Tarzan, Fantasia 2000, The Emperor's New Groove, Atlantis, Lilo & Stitch, Treasure Planet, Brother Bear,* and *Home on the Range.* Some received mild box office success, but none were hailed by critics. Worse, Disney had spent over a billion dollars making and marketing these films, yet their animation department had lost nearly $400 million during the previous ten years. The board knew things were bad, but the numbers had never been presented to them in black and white like this.

Then Iger flipped to the next slide, which displayed market research he'd been conducting. Disney's prime demographic is mothers with children under the age of twelve, so Iger had surveyed a large group of these moms from across the country and asked them to rate which movie studio produced films that were "good for their family." The results were clear. Pixar was beating Disney. Mothers loved Pixar films, while they viewed Disney as over the hill and irrelevant.

"This can't be about the past," Iger said, sensing tempers starting to rise in the room. He didn't want to point fingers or cast blame, he wanted to move forward. "There's nothing we can do about the bad creative decisions that were made and disappointing films that were released. But there's a lot we can do to change the future, and we need to start now."

Then Iger used a phrase he would return to repeatedly during the coming months.

"As Disney Animation goes, so goes the company," he said. "I feel enormous pressure to figure this out. The drum is already beating for me to solve this problem."

Iger was laying down the gauntlet, raising the stakes around the importance of fixing Disney's animated-film problem and casting it as his number one issue to address to lead the entire company forward. In so doing, he made it a Core Imperative—the highest priority of the senior management team to be addressed immediately during the current fiscal year.

He explained that he saw three possible ways to proceed. First, they could keep the current team in place, but this didn't seem likely to work. Second, they could try to bring in new blood, but he'd been searching for six months and had been unable to find the right people.

"Or," he said, "we could buy Pixar."

The room erupted into chaos at this suggestion. Everyone was suddenly talking over each other. Pixar was valued at $6 billion, someone pointed out. Steve Jobs personally owned half the company's stock, said someone else, and there's no way he would ever sell to Disney. The financials would never work out, came a third voice.

Some board members were firmly against the idea of buying Pixar, but enough were intrigued that Iger was given tentative approval to talk to Steve Jobs and Pixar's leaders, John Lasseter and Ed Catmull, about whether they might consider selling.

The next day, Iger got Jobs on the phone and asked if he could visit in a few days to discuss a crazy idea. The two men had gotten to know each other while negotiating a deal to include Disney content on Apple's new iPod Video, which was due to be released in a week.

"Tell me now," Jobs said. Iger remembered he was talking to a man who loved crazy ideas.

After putting himself on the line in front of the board, Iger was under pressure to come through. Sitting in his car after arriving home on a warm evening, he broke into a sweat as he mustered up the nerve to make his ask. Would Jobs be offended at what he was about to propose?

"I've been thinking about our respective futures," Iger said. "What do you think about the idea of Disney buying Pixar?"

For the longest time, Jobs didn't say anything. Iger winced, ready for him to erupt in anger or laugh at the arrogance of this suggestion. But that's not what happened.

"You know," Jobs said, finally, "that's not the craziest idea in the world."

Two weeks later the men met in Apple's boardroom to discuss the possibility further. Jobs was pacing up and down in front of the massive twenty-five-foot whiteboard, which took up an entire wall. He wrote "pros" on one side and "cons" on the other. Then he started jotting down one con after another:

- Disney's culture will destroy Pixar.
- Fixing Disney Animation will take too long.
- There's too much ill will and the healing will take years.
- Wall Street will hate it.
- Your board will never let you do it.
- Pixar will reject Disney as an owner, like a body rejects a donated organ.
- DISTRACTION WILL KILL PIXAR'S CREATIVITY.

The list went on, and soon Jobs had filled an entire side of the whiteboard with cons. Then he threw the marker to Iger, who struggled to come up with pros:

- Disney will be saved by Pixar and we'll all live happily ever after.

- Your team will have a much larger canvas to paint on.
- Turning Animation around will change the perception of Disney and shift our fortunes.

He couldn't think of anything else. After two hours of whiteboarding the cons vastly outnumbered the pros, and Iger was feeling dejected.

"It was a nice idea," he said meekly, "but I don't see how we do this."

That's when he learned a huge lesson from one of the most visionary thinkers of all time.

"A few solid pros are more powerful than dozens of cons," Jobs said, thoughtful. "So what should we do next?"

In the months that followed, Iger toured Pixar and met with the company's leaders, John Lasseter and Ed Catmull, to talk about what an acquisition might look like. Jobs said he wouldn't consider any offer until both of them agreed. Iger assured the two men that he didn't want to change anything about the way they worked. The deal would greatly expand their sphere of influence, placing them at the head of Disney Animation in addition to continuing to run Pixar. Their email addresses would remain Pixar. The signs in front of their headquarters would still read Pixar. They could keep all of their traditions and wacky rituals, like the "beer blasts" they held every month. Lasseter and Catmull liked the idea and gave Steve Jobs the go-ahead to enter talks with Disney about how the deal might work.

When he and his CFO, Tom Staggs, sat down with Jobs to discuss the financials, Bob Iger knew the typical approach would be to play it cool and not let on how badly he wanted this deal. The idea in this type of high-stakes negotiation is generally to avoid giving the other side any extra leverage they can use against you. If Jobs knew how excited Iger was about acquiring Pixar, he might play hardball.

But Iger took a different approach.

"I'll be straight with you," he said, as soon as they sat down. "This is something I feel we have to do." Iger's goal wasn't to get the best price possible. He just wanted the deal to be fair for both sides. He was convinced the partnership would create a massive amount of value going forward for all involved if they could just arrive at an agreement. Also, he knew Jobs couldn't ask for anything too outrageous because Disney's board would never approve it.

Jobs agreed the deal was important. He seemed to appreciate Iger's honesty.

The number they arrived at was $7.4 billion. It seemed fair to Iger—albeit on the expensive side of fair.

But the deal wasn't done yet. Iger still had to convince Disney's board of directors to sign off. He knew there was strong opposition to this deal, and to his appointment as CEO. The acquisition would involve issuing new shares of stock and diluting every current shareholder's stake in Disney. Steve Jobs would immediately become the largest shareholder and would gain a seat on the board.

The big meeting took place in January 2006 in Los Angeles. Instead of attempting to pitch the deal and convince his skeptical listeners on his own, Iger decided to bring Steve Jobs, John Lasseter, and Ed Catmull along with him to do most of the talking.

What is so interesting in this part of the story is that Bob Iger, the senior-most executive at Disney, brought in specific individuals to engage with and win over his board. Key individuals whose personal brands, market stature, experience, and vision made them exceptionally credible to deliver the intended message. They were each at least peers with the audience of Disney board members, if not singular experts, particularly on the topics they were there to address.

By leveraging Jobs, Lasseter, and Catmull to do the most important part of the pitch, not himself, Bob Iger was practicing the fine art of what I call Executive Whispering—the craft of choreographing interactions between senior executives and experts from your company and your customers. Much more to come on Executive Whispering later in the book.

*　*　*

John Lasseter spoke excitedly about his deep love for Disney, where he'd worked for years before being let go because the company didn't see a future in computerized animation. He said it would be a dream come true to return and help lead the animation team at Disney. Ed Catmull launched into an enthusiastic and highly technical talk about the future of animation and the amazing things that could be achieved from a technological standpoint with the two companies working together.

Finally, Steve Jobs took the floor. He stepped back to discuss the big picture and explained why he felt Disney had been struggling over the past ten years. He said he knew Pixar could help turn things around. He talked about the need for big companies to be bold, take risks, and pursue crazy ideas. It was a speech only Steve Jobs could pull off. And he nailed it. When he finished, the energy in the room had shifted.

"The future of the company is right here, right now," said Iger, addressing the board one final time before they voted on the deal. "It's in your hands."

Then he repeated a line he'd used during his very first board meeting as CEO, back in September. With everything that had happened since then it felt like ages ago.

"As Disney Animation goes," Iger said, "so goes the company. It was true in 1937 with *Snow White and the Seven Dwarfs*, and in 1994 with

The Lion King, and it's no less true right now. When Animation soars, Disney soars. We have to do this. Our path to the future starts right here, tonight."

The deal was approved.

Just as Iger had predicted, the Pixar acquisition was a monumental turning point for the company. Over the coming years, *Ratatouille*, *Wall-E*, *Up*, *Toy Story 3*, *Brave*, *Inside Out*, and *Coco* would all win Academy Awards for Best Animated Feature Film. The Disney-Pixar partnership created massive value all around and changed the fate of the company, exactly as Iger envisioned it would.

The acquisition of Pixar was a Mega Deal in every sense.

But Iger wasn't done yet. He went on to negotiate a string of other impressive Mega Deals during the next decade, including the purchase of Lucasfilm and the *Star Wars* franchise, as well as the acquisition of Marvel Entertainment, which brought a vast collection of beloved comic book characters under the Disney umbrella. All of these Mega Deals proved incredibly profitable, enhanced the Disney brand, and resulted in an avalanche of popular films that were adored by fans and critics alike all over the world.

Behemoth business transactions like those led by Bob Iger are certainly Mega Deals, but so are thousands of large deals that close every year, spearheaded by elite enterprise sellers. In its essence, a Mega Deal is simply an uncommonly large deal that has an outsize impact on all stakeholders who are party to the transaction.

And you don't have to be the CEO of a Fortune 500 company to close a Mega Deal. Enterprise sellers in any industry or niche can close these kinds of deals when they learn to approach the sales process in a radically different way.

I know this because I lived it. Through trial and error and ultimately through having a couple of great mentors, I learned the craft of closing very large deals. I have been fortunate enough to close over $160 million in software as a service (SaaS) and services revenue in an eight-year stretch of my career as an individual contributor account executive. Most of that revenue came through deals of $50 million and up.

Now I lead a coaching community dedicated to enabling Mega Deal practitioners. Through my work I coach or come into contact with sellers who close extraordinary deals, each with their own amazing story.

Joseph Paranteau, a friend of mine and the author of *Billion Dollar Sales Secrets*, learned this Mega Deal lesson for himself when his small software company was in the running for a contract to build a new website for American Airlines: aa.com. After months of pitches and requests for proposal (RFPs), he was stuck. The customer told him flat-out they preferred his company for their creativity and design skills, but they worried about security. There was a competing software company that had a much stronger reputation for technical architecture, a critical aspect of the proposed website.

Instead of trying to destroy his competitor, Paranteau took a different approach. Just like Bob Iger, he decided to partner with the other software company and work together on the website. The collaboration was approved and the deal ended up reaching $350 million—more than enough to go around. It was a turning point for his company and allowed his small team to shape the future of airline digital engagement and e-commerce and the way millions of people book air travel.

Anita Absey is another individual who embodies the Mega Deal mindset. In 2018, Absey was brought on as the first Chief Revenue Officer at Voxy, an e-learning company that provides institutions with adaptive instruction in English. She scaled up Voxy's sales team and spearheaded their international expansion by closing several large partnership agreements. She is convinced Voxy's product can change millions of lives for good, and she's determined to get it in the hands of as many people as possible through her extraordinary dealmaking. Like Bob Iger and Joe Paranteau, Absey focuses on deals with impact, rather than trying to get as much money out of every deal as she can. The results speak for themselves.

Mega Deals change the game for everyone involved, and they produce value on four levels:

- First, the individual seller overachieves their target by several times and is recognized for leading the effort. In Bob Iger's case, this meant he was hailed as a brilliant and visionary CEO. For Joe Paranteau, it meant he received an incredible commission check at the end of the year.
- Second, the supplier gains a marquee customer who is deeply invested in their value proposition. The aa.com deal was a huge win for Joe's company not only because it brought in $350 million, but also because it created a long-term partnership with American Airlines. This relationship was ultimately worth much more in terms of exposure and street cred than the deal itself.
- Third, the customer gets a novel capability that changes the game in some way. For Bob Iger, this meant Pixar gained the benefit of Disney's distribution resources and animation technologies. By combining forces, the companies could do more than either could alone.
- Finally, the ultimate consumers, who buy from the customer's company, experience an improvement in the quality, cost, or value. American Airlines customers benefited from the ability to book their flights online using the new automated capabilities of aa.com. Disney and Pixar customers received better movies as a result of their partnership.

This quadruple positive impact of a Mega Deal makes it a repeatable vehicle to create huge advances in productivity, efficiency, or quality of life for thousands, tens of thousands, or millions of people.

By focusing on bringing outsize value to all parties, we as sellers can overcome the negative stereotypes that have long been tied to the sales profession. We can challenge the idea that sales is a zero-sum game where one party wins and the other loses. We can shift the focus away from immediate financial gain and look instead at the measurable, positive impact a new business engagement will have for everyone involved.

Mega Deal thinking engenders purpose and meaning. Mega Dealers don't just sell widgets. We inspire change in ways that bring a better life for everyone. Since I first started writing and speaking about Mega Deals five years ago, thousands of sellers from all over the world have joined the Mega Deal movement, and you can too. Together we can transform selling from a profession to a calling. We can do something that changes the world for the better.

Leaving the Land of Run-Rate Selling

Since I started sharing what I've learned about Mega Deals, I've met thousands of enterprise sellers, many of whom sell for the biggest names in the tech world. Many express frustration with being stuck at a level of achievement far below their abilities and aspirations. They have gripes about the cutthroat world of selling and feel they are never making progress—like trying to run underwater. They are stuck in the Land of Run-Rate Selling.

The Land of Run-Rate Selling is the mental wasteland of selling to survive. It's a situation where your work is done reactively, rather than purposefully. It's predicated on the belief that if you just increase your activity, sales will follow; that you need to work fifteen opportunities at the same time; that scripted talk tracks will somehow yield signed contracts; that if you just paint by the numbers and stay within the lines then you will have success in B2B sales.

One of the worst elements of Run-Rate Selling is an overdependence on Land and Expand deals. Land and Expand is a strategy where the seller's goal is to close a small deal as fast as possible with that account with the hope of eventually growing the relationship to make bigger sales in the future.

Although the strategy has some usefulness, particularly with startups in the early stages of gaining market adoption, the Land and Expand strategy is a terrible crutch that will keep sellers poor and chasing a dream that rarely comes true.

The Run-Rate Selling mentality also causes sellers to constantly live in fear: the fear of missing your number, the fear of being fired for underperformance, the fear that this is as good as it gets for you as a seller—and what the heck are you doing with your life anyway?

These fears are all over the enterprise sales community. I've experienced them too.

When I first started studying the Mega Deal mindset, I was stuck in the Land of Run-Rate Selling myself. My sales performance was near the bottom of the heap. I'd been fired twice in a row for underperforming and was thinking about leaving sales for good.

Then something happened that changed the course of my life. Addison Kingsley, a senior seller in my business unit, closed a deal *one hundred times* bigger than usual. Our average deal at the time was $200,000. That's what we'd all been trained to close. But Addison came in, seemingly out of nowhere, and landed an account worth over $20 million. And the very next year she did another one for $36 million. Those deals not only changed the game for our sales and product teams, they also changed the game for our customers and our customers' customers. They established our product as the standard in the market and created hundreds if not thousands of new jobs in our industry. Addison gave me my first glimpse into the world of Mega Deals.

Until Addison did those two game-changing deals right in front of me, I didn't realize how small I'd been thinking. I suddenly saw I'd bought into a set of assumptions about how big (or small) a deal should be and how it should be set up. I was stuck in the Land of Run-Rate Selling, and I didn't even know it. But Addison snapped me out of it. She showed me that when you approach the customer with a radically different mindset and purpose it's possible to multiply the impact of your deals many times over.

Addison had the same job title as me and access to the same resources and contacts, but she was doing game-changing work while I was barely scraping by. What was I doing wrong? I needed to stop my myopic focus on my activity numbers, stop following the same old scripts, and start looking at my customer interactions less like repetitive transactions and more like a search for a landmark project. I needed to seek out a Big, Hairy Ambitious Goal (BHAG).

BHAGs are described in *Built to Last: Successful Habits of Visionary Companies* by Jim Collins and Jerry Porras. BHAGs are ambitious projects that rally the troops around an audacious effort and focus a team's attention on doing something truly great. It has a clear result, so everyone knows if it has been achieved or not. This powerful principle describes the impact of going after a huge enterprise deal. It's scary, it's risky, it's tricky, but the potential payoff is immense.

Inspired, I studied Addison carefully, along with a few other Mega Dealers she introduced me to. I kept notes on their methods and on what they did differently from standard sales reps. I engaged every

Mega Dealer I could find, looking for nuggets of knowledge, and a set of patterns emerged:

1. Transformative capabilities, not incremental improvement

   Mega Dealers don't pitch customers on merely improving the status quo. Instead, **they find a way to offer a revolutionary opportunity.** Mega Dealers are obsessed with looking for *massive* value. They unearth insights that shed new light on a high-priority problem or goal, and they quantify the impact they can have on the customer's business. I'll show you that process in Chapter One. Often, it takes a Mega Dealer weeks of intense research to develop a single value proposition for a new customer. Bob Iger's team spent weeks performing market research and crunching the numbers on Pixar before pitching the idea to his board, an approach typical of Mega Dealers in all industries.

2. Go straight to the top

   While typical reps won't bring a deal to their executive team until it's already in the bag, **Mega Dealers get their executives involved *early*,** from the beginning of the sales cycle. They don't waste time and energy pitching their ideas to stakeholders at the lower levels of their customers' corporate hierarchy. For Bob Iger, this meant getting Steve Jobs himself on the phone to pitch the idea, rather than floating it to Pixar through the standard channels. **Mega Dealers focus on engaging the customer's top brass: SVPs, EVPs, and even CEOs.** And there is a very specific way they go about landing these impossible meetings. More on that in Chapter Two.

3. Prove value early to avoid a small deal

Rather than the Land and Expand approach favored by countless sellers, **Mega Dealers go directly for deals of size right off the bat**. To prove their offer has the potential to provide massive value, a Mega Dealer often suggests conducting some sort of assessment (a Proof of Concept, proof of value, pilot, etc.) with the customer. The results are then used to justify the large investment the customer needs to make to achieve the desired results. For Bob Iger, this was easy because Disney and Pixar had already collaborated on successful movies like *Finding Nemo*. You'll see how to do this for yourself in Chapters Three and Four.

4. Prep for procurement

As I'll show you in Chapter Five, **a Mega Dealer develops relationships with key customer stakeholders *before* her deal ends up in procurement**. By the time she has to face down the customer's hard-nosed negotiation team, the Mega Dealer has obtained a massive amount of buy-in, goodwill, and leverage. She is able to stand her ground confidently during negotiations because she knows her offer is distinctive, she has clear data demonstrating its value, and she already has support from key stakeholders, in some cases right up to the CEO. With so much momentum behind the deal, procurement is unable to isolate the rep, commoditize the offering, and drive the price down. When executed properly, which I will discuss in Chapter Six, this system leaves procurement with significantly fewer paths to challenge the terms and price set by the Mega Dealer.

Learning how to structure and close Mega Deals is an opportunity to differentiate yourself in the eyes of your customers. Because so few sellers even attempt to pursue them, there is actually *less* competition for Mega Deals than for smaller ones. The vast majority of sellers have no idea how to put together a transformational customer engagement. Many don't believe it's possible for them or their offering. This widely held belief presents a green field of opportunity for anyone with the audacity to think big and the tenacity to learn and apply the Mega Deal craft.

Mega Deals: Not Just for Superhero Sellers

I need to dispel a myth here—an assumption I bought into for years. When I first saw Addison do her deals, I thought I could never reach that level. Her numbers were so far above mine that I could not fathom how she did it, nor did I see how I could ever come close to that level of achievement myself. I saw her as a mythical figure far above the rest of us mere mortals.

The truth is that Mega Deals are not just for superhero sellers. I have learned that the people who close uncommonly large transactions are not inherently more talented or capable than the rest of us. Mega Deals are for normal sellers like you and me who learn the methods, change their mindset, and stick to it with unwavering determination.

My own story proves this point. I am certainly not a superhero. I've had more failures than successes. I have been fired twice (in a row) for underperformance in sales. During my first decade as a seller, my performance was extremely average. I even look average. My forehead is too big. I'm terrible at calculating numbers in my head. I've never been a flamboyant seller or hard closer, and I hate cold outreach, scripted pitching, and aggressive negotiating.

And yet, somehow, despite all my failures and averageness, I was able to close the three largest deals of the decade among my employers—some of which had thousands of sales reps.

I learned the art of the Mega Deal.

In the pages that follow, you too will learn every step of the Mega Deal process—from selecting the right candidate account and finding a Distinctive Value Proposition to getting your contract signed by whatever deadline you set. You'll see how I put together the biggest pitch of my career, stood my ground with the most intimidating executive I've ever met, and, ultimately, closed my first Mega Deal.

Along the way, you'll meet a full cast of real-life Mega Deal characters, including:

- **Giovanni Lamere:** My jet-setting Italian VP of Sales with a mind like a computer, who often called me at 3:00 a.m. while riding his motorcycle
- **Arun Baines:** My VP of Professional Services, a lanky, pensive, longtime industry player and academic, born in San Francisco, with roots in Delhi
- **Gunther Svedel:** The stone-faced executive who pushed me to my limits but ultimately became a supporter
- **Bill McClellan:** An EVP who agreed to help with my deal, then decided to wing it all by himself during the most important meeting of my life
- **Vlad Malik:** A paperwork whiz who knew every type of approval and exception process at my company and saved my bacon multiple times
- **Victor Boliche:** Our company's top-secret negotiator who only worked on the very biggest deals and had an unlisted, untraceable phone number and no email address

Settle in for an over-the-shoulder look into the deal of my life.

CHAPTER 1

THE MEGA DEAL PREMISE

The biggest deal of my life is falling apart before my eyes, I thought, my mouth suddenly dry, as Gunther glared at me angrily from across the table.

"You don't understand," Gunther said, his voice dripping with exasperation. "This isn't about working out a discount. Or adding a few extra buttons to your software. **This is about protecting the most important intellectual property in the entire company.**" His piercing blue eyes cut through his thick-rimmed spectacles, and he tapped his foot impatiently, ruffling the crisp fabric of his charcoal suit. To his right and left sat members of his team. Next to me were my two bosses, Giovanni and Arun.

I had no idea what Gunther was talking about.

"You're right," I stalled. "I can see why you're frustrated. I would be too." Gunther relaxed slightly. I pressed: "Can you explain what, specifically, we must do to take better care of that intellectual property? How would that look on your end?"

"Safer and faster," he said.

Very helpful, I thought to myself.

"My neck is on the line if we don't get this done right," Gunther shot back. "Everyone above me here—the senior vice president, the EVP, the CEO—they all want to make sure we have safe hands on the intellectual property of the company. And that is not happening here. I'm sorry to say it, but given the situation, we have started to explore alternative providers."

My career flashed before my eyes. It was my first meeting since being assigned to this account, and I was already losing the contract. "All right." I nodded again. I didn't know what else to say. Gunther had taken away every piece of leverage in my arsenal. Normally I would offer a discount or extra features, but he'd wiped those options off the table.

"I'll do everything I can to fix this and get some safer hands on the IP," I said cautiously. "I need more time to investigate and work out a plan. And I'll need access to your crash lab so I can gain a deeper understanding of the process and what's going wrong."

Gunther considered. He narrowed his eyes.

"Well . . ." He nodded. "Let's meet again in three weeks to review your proposal, Jamal. I'll get you access to the lab."

Moments later, Arun, Giovanni, and I were piling into the back of the limousine. Frustrated and spent, I'd ripped off my jacket and thrown it in the trunk with the rest of our bags. Underneath, I was drenched in sweat. As usual, Giovanni was whistling to himself and Arun was lost in thought, staring out the window.

Arun didn't say much—ever. He was a tall and gaunt PhD statistician whose parents immigrated from the West Indies to San Francisco in the sixties. Most of the time he looked as though he was busy thinking hard about something very deep and complex. He always wore the same tweed jacket and corduroys.

Giovanni was, in many ways, the polar opposite of Arun. Short and stocky with a round, ruddy face, bushy black mustache, warm smile, and fierce eyes, he was the son of an Italian brain surgeon and a French landscape painter. Giovanni grew up in Genoa and studied electrical engineering at Cambridge, where he was also captain of the rugby team. His ears were scarred and cauliflowered from years of being repeatedly whacked in the head. Now Giovanni was single-handedly responsible for overseeing dozens of our largest active contracts, totaling well over half a billion dollars.

In addition to his unconventional appearance and impressive business accolades, Giovanni intrigued me to no end because he was incredibly sophisticated and cultured. He was always ready to strike up a jovial debate about anything under the sun, including, but not limited to, politics, economics, sixteenth-century paintings, jazz and blues of the 1920s, a Napa Cab versus a French Bordeaux, Russian literature, or the lyrics of Nicki Minaj. Independently wealthy since long before he came to work for us, Giovanni owned four homes, scattered in various remote regions around the globe—all of which he'd designed and built himself from scratch. He spent most of his time riding high-speed motorcycles, sailing the world, flying his airplanes, and, occasionally, swooping in to help our company negotiate and close a huge contract. Then . . . poof! He would disappear again.

"I'm worried," Arun mused as the driver pulled away from the curb and turned toward the airport. "Even if we do fix the IP issues, I feel the contract could get smaller. Gunther seems wary to sign on for another three years of this."

"Are you joking?" Giovanni was incredulous. "Were we just in the same room? That meeting changed everything for us! I now think this deal is worth more than $10 million. Much more."

"What do you mean?" I asked.

"Did you hear what he said?" Giovanni continued. "'This is not about discounts.' He said this is the most important intellectual property their company owns. He needs a big result; therefore, he opened the door for us to bring him a big solution. He told us Enginex has a massive problem. This is no longer a simple renewal. This is a red alert request for assistance—a massive opportunity."

Giovanni was right. I'd been looking at this situation all wrong. I should have been celebrating, not moping. It was great that Enginex had a problem with their current provider—even if the provider was us! This gave us an opening to craft an ambitious solution. I understood Giovanni's vision; we might be able to expand the deal, but before we had any hope of that, we'd need to fix the intellectual property issues once and for all. And, before that was possible, I had to figure out what the issues were and what was causing them.

It wasn't going to be easy, but for the first time in months I felt excitement in addition to my nagging sense of dread. The situation wasn't as hopeless as I'd thought.

"And if we do fix their 'audacious problem,'" I asked, leaning forward, trying to keep the eagerness out of my voice, "how big could this deal be?"

"Very large," he said, stroking his chin as he thought. "I think this is a Victor-level deal."

"Ah yes." Arun nodded thoughtfully. "I agree. Victor would be quite interested."

"Who is Victor?" I asked. Giovanni smiled mysteriously.

"The James Bond of Mega Deals," he said.

* * *

When I first walked into that meeting with Gunther, I was stuck in the Land of Run-Rate Selling. I was focused on pacifying the customer and salvaging our existing contract, even if we had to offer significant discounts. If I could make them happy enough to renew this year, I figured I might be able to push for a larger deal down the road. It was classic Land and Expand thinking. Giovanni helped me start to think like a Mega Dealer. He showed me that Enginex was a perfect target for a large, transformational deal because they were experiencing massive pain around an issue their senior leadership cared about.

Finding a Mega Deal Candidate Account

It's possible to close a deal ten times the size of anything you've ever done—but you can't do it with your current process. When Bob Iger sold his board of directors on the idea of buying Pixar, he wasn't using any kind of standard sales methodology. He sold a vision of the future. Don't expect to use your current approach to attract and close significantly larger deals. It doesn't work that way. By definition, if you are used to closing small deals, your existing process is a small deal process. You've been trained to solve a small problem for a lower-level customer stakeholder. This book is about how to replace that with a Mega Deal process, where you'll solve a major problem for a customer executive.

The vast majority of enterprise sellers engage low-level customer stakeholders and close smaller deals. Mega Dealers are hyper-focused on senior stakeholders and executives. Working your way up the chain of command from the bottom is a long journey fraught with perils and political maneuvering. By approaching executives directly, Mega Dealers skip that entire chapter of the book. When you reach the senior level of management, the conversations are so different compared with those with worker bees or middle management. In my experience, the more senior the player you engage, the less they hesitate to share internal pains or block your access to other key players. It feels like that moment on an airplane when you reach your cruising altitude, the turbulence of takeoff subsides, and the seat belt sign turns off. *You are now free to move about the cabin.*

The first step in putting together a Mega Deal is selecting the right candidate account. You want to look for a potential customer with a big problem that you can help solve. Decades of research on cognitive biases has confirmed that avoiding losses is more impactful than achieving gains. Studies show people will work two to three times harder to avoid losing a dollar than we will to earn a new dollar. While every company wants to increase revenue and make more money, they are even more motivated to avoid losing money. To make a Mega Deal happen, look among your top accounts to find a large company that is obviously going through significant pain in an area that your solution can address. Don't worry if you don't have every detail yet. Do your best discovery within the account to find the big, obvious pains and follow your gut on which account you will invest in as a Mega Deal candidate.

When Bob Iger realized Disney Animation had lost $400 million over the past decade and their brand was being eclipsed by Pixar among their target demographic, he realized he might have an opportunity to pitch the "crazy idea" of buying Pixar to his board of directors. Similarly, when Giovanni, Arun, and I learned that Enginex considered their crash test data to be their most important intellectual property, we realized they had a burning desire to stop it from being mishandled.

That made them a perfect Mega Deal candidate, even though they were frustrated with our service at the time.

Among your accounts, which would you consider a Mega Deal candidate?

Mega Deals can be done with current customers or net new accounts. However, I prioritize existing customers when looking for Mega Deal candidate accounts—relationships exist and master agreements are already in place. Disney had already partnered with Pixar on numerous films in the past, and Bob Iger already had a relationship with Steve Jobs from negotiating the iPod Video deal. Similarly, I had a smaller contract in place with Enginex when we saw the opportunity to radically increase the scope of our engagement. The quickest path to a Mega Deal is through your existing customers, but it's not about making small improvements to their existing contracts. A Mega Deal is about offering your customer an entirely new way to collaborate around an ambitious endeavor that goes well beyond the business you're already doing together.

Starting with one of your current customers will speed everything up, regardless of whether the customer is happy or in crisis. It may be counterintuitive, but sometimes an unhappy customer can be a great Mega Deal candidate because they have that all-important characteristic we touched on earlier: they are experiencing massive *pain*. That means they are in a state of readiness to make a big change. By offering a unique way to stop the pain, you can transform their negative reality into a positive future. My first Mega Deal customer, Enginex Testing, was in exactly that situation. We were on their "worst vendor ever" list because our inadequate solution was causing them pain. Hundreds of users were complaining about problems using our platform. That immense pain, *even though it stemmed from my own solution*, gave me an opportunity to pitch something vastly better.

You might not have an existing customer with Mega Deal potential. In that case, look to the largest prospect accounts in your territory. In general, it's easier to sell something truly Mega to a larger company because they have bigger problems and more resources, but there are certainly exceptions where smaller companies have a strategic need for major investment.

Despite all the creative cold outreach strategies available today, nothing beats a warm introduction. Bob Iger didn't rely on cold outreach to engage with Pixar; he already had a relationship with their top decision maker and was immediately able to get Steve Jobs on the phone.

But you don't have to be a Fortune 500 CEO to get a warm introduction to someone who can make your Mega Deal happen. The top channels for brokering warm introductions are:

Members of Your Network: Mega Dealers are perpetual networkers. You should always be looking to connect with people of capacity. Go out of your way to deliver value to influential people, even when you don't specifically need anything in return. In fact, that's the best time to establish new relationships because you will be offering value to a new contact with no expectations of reciprocity. There's a great book that gets into the detail of how best to perpetually build your network, *Dig Your Well Before You're Thirsty: The Only Networking Book You'll Ever Need* by Harvey Mackay. This practice requires time and effort, but it pays off for years to come. At some point you'll be able to leverage your ever-growing network to connect with people you'd like to reach.

Executives: The executives at your own company are an important but often overlooked source of warm introductions. These individuals typically have years of experience in your industry and have inevitably built up sizeable networks of their own. They are also very motivated to leverage their networks to help drive new business. When you are searching for your next

Mega Deal candidate account, it's a good idea to sit down with a few of your execs and do a "who do you know" exercise.

Board Members and Advisors: Your company's board members and advisors are likely senior executives in the mature stages of their careers. This means they usually have a world-class network, sometimes sitting on several boards simultaneously. They are a wealth of opportunity for warm introductions and are often overlooked by enterprise sellers because they seem out of reach.

Depending on the size of your company, accessing board members or advisors should be doable if you approach it in the right way and get buy-in from your management chain to introduce you. I have engaged board members in the past, with the support of my CEO, and the results have been outstanding. Not only have they been able to quickly open doors with very senior players in my accounts, their market knowledge has also been instrumental in making sure my messaging is on point.

One word of caution: before you engage your board members, make sure you are fully prepared for any interaction with them. Treat them as you would any C-level executive; have a briefing document ready to help contextualize why you're targeting a given account, and lay out all the intel you've gathered to date. Also, don't overstep in terms of asking for too much involvement or too many introductions. Their time is valuable; use it efficiently for 10x results.

Customer Executives: Some of your current customers may have executives who would be willing to introduce you to other prospective customers. These introductions are valuable and rare. Even if they love your offering and have success with it, many executives will be hesitant to make an introduction for you because they guard their networks closely. However, some *will* be OK making a call for you, and when you find them, they are gold. It doesn't get much better than when a happy customer executive refers you to a senior stakeholder within another account.

Partners: Another great way to get a warm introduction to a prime Mega Deal candidate is through a partnership. In most tech or professional services companies there will be someone on staff with a title like Head of Partnerships or VP of Channels & Alliances. Go to this person and ask which consulting partners your company has relationships with. There are a handful of large consulting firms, such as McKinsey & Company, Deloitte, Accenture, Ernst & Young, Boston Consulting Group, and Capgemini. Large corporations often hire these firms to help execute new projects and initiatives. The senior people at these firms have worked with executives at virtually every Fortune 100 company. Beyond the big players named above, there are thousands of smaller consulting shops that are routinely looking for good providers to partner with.

Mega Dealers approach partner organizations by going straight to the top whenever possible. There will generally be a lower- or mid-level contact within the partner organization assigned to your company, but working with them exclusively exposes you to a lack of decision-making authority. Senior players within the partner organization have the greatest likelihood of being close to top executives within your candidate account. Like board members or advisors, they can not only provide a warm introduction but also help round out your understanding of issues the customer faces and refine your value proposition.

Other Enterprise Sellers: If you work for a large company, there may be sellers in other business units who can help you get close to a new customer. Sometimes when you're targeting a really big account you can work as a team to combine products and craft a more complete solution and, thus, a bigger Mega Deal. Spend time with other reps who sell related products to the same accounts as you do, and brainstorm about how your respective offerings might be able to solve bigger problems together rather than separately.

There are many ways to get connected to potential Mega Deal customers, but the factors to look for remain the same. The perfect candidate for a Mega Deal is an account with a big problem to solve and the will and budget to solve it. You also need the ability to gain a warm introduction to someone senior at the target company.

The Opportunity Takes Shape

Tires screeched and the sound of glass, metal, and plastic smashing against concrete echoed through the early-morning air, but the street was deserted in both directions except for Victor and me. Dark warehouses lined the block on either side of us. I looked at the blue dot in the center of my phone screen. This was the place. The unmarked building in front of us was the Enginex crash-testing lab. The information I needed was inside.

I snuck a glance at Victor, still finding it hard to believe I was standing next to a man who had closed over $10 billion worth of business. He was our company's top negotiation expert, the James Bond of Mega Deals. Except Victor Boliche didn't look like a Hollywood action hero, he looked like a linebacker.

"Good morning," he boomed as we stepped into the reception area. "I've got Jamal Reimer here, from Zerlegen. He should be on the list."

"Sure," said the receptionist. "Let me check."

She produced a sheet, stamped it, and moved it to a different pile.

"Here he is," she said. "I've got him checked in. And who are you? I don't see a guest listed."

I'd been wondering how Victor was going to handle this. Gunther said he'd put *me* on the list, but he hadn't mentioned anything about bringing a guest. On the ride over, when I'd brought this up, Victor simply waved his fingers as if there wouldn't be a problem. Now he was being challenged, just as I'd anticipated.

"I'm Victor Boliche," he thundered, his voice rumbling from deep in his chest. "Legal counsel, here to accompany Jamal."

I have never seen a human being with a better poker face than Victor Boliche. He stood perfectly still, stone-faced, towering over the receptionist and staring into her. There wasn't a hint of malice in his features, nor any trace of warmth. He was just . . . blank.

After a tense and wordless moment, the receptionist shrank backward. Victor didn't move. She mumbled something about strict policies and tight security. But even as she did she nodded her head, reached for the buzzer, and waved us through the massive steel doors.

Dang, this guy is good, I thought to myself as Victor and I stepped through the top-secret entrance to the Enginex crash lab.

No sooner had we crossed over the threshold than, once again, came the sound of rubber screeching against pavement and a car smashing against concrete. Somewhere in this building, metal was crumpling, glass was shattering, plastic and leather were being vaporized under the force of a high-speed collision.

Then an alarm buzzed and excited voices filled the air.

We were walking down a long, dark hallway. On either side, soundproof doors demarcated entrances to various offices. Engineering. Logistics. Budgeting. One door in particular, Data Analytics, caught our attention. Peering through the small round window, however, we saw the room was dark and deserted. We kept walking toward the end of the hall, where a large set of stainless-steel double doors loomed, a red siren light flashing above them.

CRASH LAB was stenciled across the doors in red spray paint.

We reached the end of the hall, and Victor pushed through the doors confidently. I followed close behind.

Inside was a massive warehouse with shiny white floors and a line of pillars supporting a towering ceiling. Crossing the room was a long runway with concrete blocks at one end and a brand-new convertible sports car at the other. Cameras, sensors, and high-tech devices lay everywhere, with a complex web of cables and wires running all over the place.

Off to the side, a group of technicians in lab coats and safety goggles gestured to a bank of monitors, talking excitedly. Another team was cleaning up the mangled remains of the crash we'd heard a moment prior. Occasionally one of the techs would yell to the others, and they would all gather around, pointing and taking photos. Then they'd go back to cleaning up the wreckage.

One man wasn't helping with the work. He held a clipboard under his arm and strolled with authority, barking orders. Victor raised an eyebrow. This was the boss.

The boss spotted us hanging around by the door and glided over, curious. A couple techs saw us too and followed after him.

"How can I help you?" asked the boss. "Touring the facility?"

"Yes," I responded. "Jamal Reimer from Zerlegen. We build the statistical models for the data you generate here. I understand there are problems with the way your intellectual property has been handled, and Gunther sent us over to get a better idea of what's wrong and how to fix it."

The man looked thoughtfully from me to Victor. Finally, he nodded to the two techs who had followed him over.

"Valdez, Dornier," he said. "Walk these fellas through our design and fabrication process and show them where Zerlegen has been dropping the ball on the regulatory reports. Just don't give away anything proprietary, all right?"

"Sure, boss," said the shorter of the two, Dornier. And with that the boss spun around and marched off, leaving the four of us alone. As soon as he was gone, Dornier cracked a smile. "Sorry about Heff," he said. "He's always got a stick up his backside. Nothing personal. Come on, we'll show you over to des/fab."

We followed Valdez and Dornier through a door labeled Design & Fabrication. The vibe inside felt more like a startup than an industrial manufacturing and testing facility. Calming scents of bergamot and eucalyptus filled the air. The walls featured inspirational words like "synergy," "ambiance," "passion," and "teamwork." Engineers sat on Herman Miller ergonomic chairs at open workstations.

In the center of the room a large 3-D printer hummed away.

"We have a few guys on-site at each major car manufacturer," Dornier was saying. "Those companies won't let the full plans for a new model leave the grounds. Our engineers work up preliminary specs for every component and communicate the requirements back to our team here. Then we design and prototype the parts in-house and run tests for durability under simulated weather conditions."

We kept walking. I was hanging on every word, hoping for any clues that would help me close this deal. We spilled through another set of doors and into a room filled with testing chambers, which looked like high-tech fish tanks. Each contained a car component undergoing testing. In one I saw a door handle submerged in water. In another was a brake pad coated with ice. Displays above each tank revealed the temperature, humidity, barometric pressure, and hours left in the test.

"That's only the first ten days," said Valdez as we walked between the tanks. "From the time our engineers get access to the plans on-site we have ten days to provide preliminary designs to the manufacturer. The timeline isn't negotiable because every extra day increases the risk of missing a regulatory deadline and getting fined."

That caught my attention. When Gunther said we needed to be "faster" with Enginex's intellectual property, maybe that's what he was referring to. In the crash-testing business, I realized, every day counted.

"Right," Dornier agreed, tapping his security card to open the next door. "Then they send out prototype vehicles. We get those twelve to fourteen days later. During that time, we continue to test and improve the designs, and we get fifty sets manufactured at full durability."

He flipped on the lights. We were standing in a warehouse containing four double-decker transport trailers, each holding ten identical convertible sports cars.

"Then they show up here." Valdez shrugged. "And we have a week to install the updated components and crash test fifty cars."

We walked by the cars, which were stamped with Top Secret, Crash Test Model Only, Property of Enginex Testing, and Not for Resale.

"The data from the tests is uploaded to your servers immediately," Valdez continued, leading us to yet another secure door. "Your analysts then have eight days to complete the report in order for us to meet our deadline and submit the results to the regulatory board for approval."

Passing through the next door, we found ourselves back in the main crash lab. The wreckage had been cleared, and the techs were preparing another sports car for annihilation.

"That's it," Dornier said. "Just in time to see the next test. Come on."

He waved us toward the semicircle of screens and monitors where the other techs were gathering to watch the crash.

"Hold on," I said. "What happens if our analysts miss the eight-day deadline?"

"That would be a big deal," said Valdez. "We'd be fined $10 million if we miss a deadline. Knock on wood, you've never missed a deadline yet. But the submissions from your analysts are getting slower lately. We're getting closer to missing one."

I stopped in my tracks. Every missed deadline cost Enginex *$10 million*? Even Victor, the man with the stone-cold poker face, did a double take.

That was our golden ticket.

An alarm buzzed and lights flashed. Our hosts headed over toward the mob of other techs. I was looking forward to witnessing my first crash test. But now I was even more excited to get back to the office. My mind was spinning. I finally understood the problems with this account. Giovanni was right. If every missed deadline cost Enginex $10 million—and there could potentially be several missed deadlines— they would certainly be open to an innovative solution. We'd found a problem big enough for a Mega Deal. Now we had to find a way to eliminate the delays.

As we headed after Valdez and Dornier, Victor looked back at me, smiled, and flashed a subtle thumbs-up.

We'd gotten what we came for.

The techs all counted down together in unison, "Five. Four. Three. Two. One!" Then the car accelerated along the track, wires hanging out the window, cameras flashing, and sirens blaring. I shook my head, marveling at the process. The techs threw their hands in the air and cheered.

*   *   *

During my initial meeting with Gunther I learned better management of the company's intellectual property was a big priority. However, I didn't understand what that meant. All I'd been able to get out of Gunther was that we needed to be "safer and faster," which wasn't very specific. When I visited the crash lab, however, I discovered Enginex was fined \$10 million for missing regulatory deadlines. Further, I was told we'd been turning our reports in later and a missed deadline was becoming increasingly likely. Now I knew exactly what problem I needed to solve for a shot at a Mega Deal with Enginex.

The Mega Deal Premise

Imagine arriving at the headquarters of your biggest potential customer, stepping into the elevator, and finding yourself face-to-face with their CEO. The two of you are alone. She presses a button and the door closes. You have twelve seconds before she'll reach her floor and get off. What do you say?

"Hi."

"Good morning."

"Great elevators you have here."

"I love your jacket."

"No elevator music?"

"Your lobby has great feng shui."

Most of us would say nothing. Or at least nothing important. We might sputter out a few trivialities and plaster a dorky grin across our faces. Maybe glance down at the trusty smartphone to save us from having to say anything at all.

Why do we do this?

Or, more importantly, why *don't* we approach and engage senior customer executives? Most of the time it's because we don't have a unique and compelling business opportunity to offer them. We haven't put in the effort to discover a pain, gap, inefficiency, risk, or opportunity the customer doesn't already know about. When Bob Iger stood in front of his board for his very first meeting as CEO of Disney, he revealed data they had never seen before, showing they were losing money and their brand was slipping. He started off by pointing out a pain point they weren't aware of yet.

The key to closing the biggest deals is to find a new way to create a massive impact for your customers. Until you think big and find a unique way to deliver distinctive value, you'll never have anything to say in that elevator to get the CEO's attention. So how do you find your distinctive value?

You need a **Mega Deal Premise, an opportunity to solve a significant problem or achieve an ambitious desire that senior customer stakeholders deeply care about**. The Mega Deal Premise has three main parts:

1. **Core Imperative:** One of your customer's most important goals
2. **C-Level Insight:** A new piece of information that reveals how or why your customer is experiencing pain and having trouble achieving their goal

3. **Distinctive Value Proposition:** A clear story demonstrating that *only* your offering can help the customer reduce the pain and achieve their goal

The Mega Deal Premise is the backbone of a Mega Deal pursuit. It is what will intrigue customer stakeholders from the very first meeting and gain you the green light to move forward with the deal. It will form the bedrock of your return on investment calculations and help you justify the size of your deal.

You'll refer back to your Mega Deal Premise throughout the sales cycle to enhance motivation and steer the conversation. These three elements will also be your best tools to successfully navigate price negotiations and avoid procurement's roadblocks. Once you identify a candidate account and establish your Core Imperative, C-Level Insight, and Distinctive Value Proposition, you'll be ready to pursue a Mega Deal.

The Core Imperative

Core Imperatives are like vital organs. **They are the highest priority goals and initiatives your customer's C-suite executives are focused on** *this fiscal year.*

In 1979, Intel, the world's largest semiconductor manufacturer, faced an existential threat that quickly formed their one and only Core Imperative: beat Motorola.

In late November of 1979, a District Manager named Don Buckout sent an urgent message to management that confirmed the worst— Intel's sixteen-bit microprocessor, the 8086, was getting thrashed in the market by Motorola's 68000. News quickly reached Intel CEO Andy Grove, who immediately raised an all-hands alarm. Soon Marketing

Manager Jim Lally raised the battle cry companywide and set the tone for the year:

> There's only one company competing with us, and that's Motorola. The 68000 is the competition. We have to kill Motorola, that's the name of the game. We have to crush the f-king bastards. We're gonna roll over Motorola and make sure they don't come back again.

Intel management set about refocusing the entire company around the Core Imperative of dominating the microprocessor market specifically by winning the battle between their 8086 and Motorola's 68000.

The first step in building a compelling Mega Deal Premise is to locate a Core Imperative. You need to find a goal your customer cares deeply about. Core Imperatives tend to be tied to performance, such as:

- **Bank of America:** "Our corporate target is to provide annual earnings per share growth in excess of 10 percent."
- **Google:** "We aim to be the first major company to achieve 24/7 carbon-free energy by 2030."
- **Cisco:** "[We aim to achieve] our target of 50% of revenue from software and services."

Hunt for Core Imperatives on the company's investor relations websites, where you can find annual reports and transcripts or replays of analyst calls. Also, watch for any relevant stories in the general media. Executive interviews on podcasts, Bloomberg News, and CNBC can be helpful too. And many executives post on Twitter and LinkedIn about corporate projects and initiatives.

One of the sellers whom I have coached, Ron Masi, had Disney in his territory. He researched all the interviews of Bob Iger he could find on YouTube. He then collected clips of Iger talking about Disney's need to establish a more direct relationship with their customers: moviegoing families. Ron filmed a short video in which he drew on a whiteboard and laid out a framework for how his solution could enable Disney to connect directly with their audience. He then distributed the video by email to members of his deal team and management to gain their buy-in to pursue Disney as a customer. Ron had identified a Core Imperative for Disney's CEO. He was gearing up his team for a Mega Deal.

In addition to public information, there are also more direct sources that can help you uncover Core Imperatives. Lower-level contacts within an account can tune you in to the customer's top priorities. So can other sales reps who share the same account for other products or services. Partners are also a great source of insights into a customer's Core Imperatives. If you get connected with senior people at the right partner firms you can often find the exact consultants who worked with the customer to shape their Core Imperatives in the first place.

One of the best places to look when you're digging for Core Imperatives is among former customer employees. Their knowledge of the organization will be fresh, and they are often open to sharing their perspectives on key players, priorities, and how to work with the company.

The most common Core Imperatives for Mega Deals are centered around business transformations, three- to five-year plans, and mission-critical initiatives or crises (data breaches, regulatory failures, and imminent threats). Don't try to build your Mega Deal Premise around a goal the company isn't already pursuing. Your job as a Mega Dealer is to close uncommonly large deals as fast as possible. You won't be able to convince a customer to drop everything and adopt a new Core Imperative in the current fiscal year. Build your Mega Deal around a Core Imperative the customer is already focused on.

For Bob Iger, when he was trying to sell his board on buying Pixar, he centered his pitch around a white-hot Core Imperative: address the failures of Disney Animation because "as Animation goes, so goes the company." He knew the only way he was going to get the board to invest over $7 billion in buying Pixar was to convince them the acquisition was their best shot at avoiding an existential threat: the loss of their flagship product line—animated films. That was Disney's greatest Core Imperative.

C-Level Insights

When you've located one of your customer's Core Imperatives, the next step is to develop your C-Level Insight.

A C-Level Insight is a new discovery or way of thinking about what stands between the customer's current state and the achievement of one of their Core Imperatives. A C-Level Insight is a critical part of a Mega Deal Premise. To understand why that is the case, we need to take a step back and look at how enterprise purchases are made today.

One of the most talked about sales books in recent history is *The Challenger Sale: Taking Control of the Customer Conversation* by Matthew Dixon and Brent Adamson. Two key learnings from the book are:

1. The most consistently successful sellers challenge their customers to think differently about their challenges and aspirations.
2. Rock star sellers do not lead with questions. They lead with insights.

As the authors describe in *The Challenger Sale*, customers often have no idea how to improve their business. "What if customers' single greatest need—ironically—is to figure out exactly what they need?" they asked. "When you get right down to it, Challengers aren't so much world-class investigators as they are world-class teachers. They win not by understanding their customers' world as well as the customers know it themselves, but by actually knowing their customers' world better than their customers know it themselves, teaching them what they don't know but should." (*The Challenger Sale*, p. 45)

Dixon and Adamson's research shows that customers who become loyal buyers, who will buy more over time and who will sing the praises of their supplier, respond to sellers who help them learn important things they didn't already know. Such sellers offer unique perspectives and help customers navigate alternative ways to solve problems and avoid costly mistakes. Most of all, they educate customers about new ways of attacking problems and achieving results.

Every one of these characteristics of super-successful rep behavior is a different way to deliver insights.

In today's selling environment most buyers have grown tired of being questioned to death. Don't get me wrong, going through a thorough discovery process is absolutely part of the process, but customers don't appreciate being peppered with questions like "What keeps you up at night?" and "What are your biggest projects this year?" These are tired questions that signal to buyers that the seller has not done his homework and is looking to the customer to spend their time to educate the rep. The essence of the research findings in *The Challenger Sales* is that we should behave exactly the opposite. The role of the modern seller is to bring business insights that are timely, relevant, valuable, actionable, and *new*. No one likes to hear a repeat performance of a presentation they have already heard weeks before. And no one likes to feel they are being asked questions to give a rep ammo that will be used to aggressively sell a widget to them.

The magic of the right insight is in its simplicity: it is an intriguing story that articulates the nature of the customer's problem in a simple yet profound way. It is sometimes counterintuitive or discovered from an unlikely source within the customer's organization. It takes the customer on a journey to their promised land, the achievement of a Core Imperative. And on this journey, the only way to get there is by using your solution as the vehicle.

If you share an insight about a pain point the C-suite is ready to invest in but your insight yields a scenario that can be solved in multiple ways, the customer will want to go get bids from multiple potential providers and look for the best price they can get. The goal is not only to find a new truth about a problem or opportunity but also to demonstrate that the best response to the insight is something that can be addressed by your solution *better than any alternative.*

The task of uncovering a truly meaningful insight is not easy. It takes work, research, team effort, and collaboration with your customer. If finding a C-Level Insight was simple, there would be many more people out there closing Mega Deals. This is really difficult and time-consuming.

To find a C-Level Insight, you start from one of your customer's Core Imperatives. Not all insights are created equal. You need an insight that will be compelling to senior management. A low-level insight might shed light on a minor inefficiency, offering a 10 percent improvement. A higher-level insight could identify an opportunity to cut resource usage by 35 percent. But the most valuable type of insight will reveal a transformational way of solving one of their biggest problems, and it could yield 10x returns. Even still, you might reveal an amazing insight that can be perfectly addressed by your offering, but if it's not square in the middle of an issue senior management is focused on this year, you'll get a "that's great, but it's not a priority for us right now" response. Or else you'll be passed off to talk with someone much lower in the customer's organization without a mandate to be taken seriously.

You need to tell Intel a secret about how they can beat Motorola.

On the Enginex account, I first realized the potential for a C-Level Insight when Gunther said, "Everyone above me here—the senior vice president, the EVP, the CEO—they all want to make sure we have safe hands on the intellectual property of the company." This tipped me off to the fact that safeguarding intellectual property was a Core Imperative for Enginex. That's why I journeyed to the crash lab and started poking around. I was looking to uncover something critical about Enginex's data safeguarding problems that their C-suite wasn't aware of yet.

The lives of senior executives are hectic and overloaded—a constant stream of calls and meetings from morning to night. Everyone wants their time. To get an executive's attention and rise above the noise, your insight must hit the bull's-eye in terms of Core Imperatives and it must be *captivating*.

In *Insight Selling*, Mike Schultz and John Doerr recommend finding insights by conducting brainstorming sessions with customer executives. That can certainly work, if you can get some of your customer executives to volunteer their time to help you figure out the best way to sell your product to their company. In *The Challenger Sale*, Dixon and Adamson advocate Hypothesis-Based Selling, whereby the seller generates the insight based on experience and research.

With either approach, the ideas must feel fresh—not recycled ideas they have heard from a conga line of management consultants. You need to trigger an aha moment where your audience can quickly digest the new discovery you researched or tested or stumbled upon to reveal a previously unknown truth about the nature of the problem and more importantly *how to fix it*. Whatever process you use to generate your C-Level Insight, it is a key component of building your Mega Deal Premise. The insight brings clarity to why the customer is having trouble achieving a Core Imperative and at least hope, if not outright proof, that the pain is indeed curable.

For Bob Iger, the insight was simple: Disney's recent movies weren't very good. The characters weren't memorable. Pixar was out-innovating them in terms of both storytelling and animation technology, proven by their tremendous success at the box office. He revealed the massive losses the company was experiencing and explained why they were having these problems. Iger then shared his aha moment with the board by telling how he realized the depth of Disney Animation's decline through the story about the parade floats.

With Enginex I was getting close to uncovering a C-Level Insight when I learned missed deadlines cost the company $10 million each. But I wasn't quite there yet. I still needed to figure out *why* we were coming so close to missing the deadlines. I needed a compelling story about what was causing the problems, and how my offering could be the best alternative to fix them.

The Distinctive Value Proposition

A Core Imperative and C-Level Insight by themselves aren't enough to sell your Mega Deal. **You also need a plan for how your customer can take advantage of the insight using your solution.** You're not doing this research and revealing this insight to show how smart you are. The goal is to close a Mega Deal. To do that, you must show the customer a solution in which they are willing to heavily invest.

The Distinctive Value Proposition should highlight the unique or distinctive aspects of your solution. You don't want the customer to act on your insight by taking a competitor's offer. You want to inspire them to work with you and you alone. So you need to show them something distinctive about your solution they can't get anywhere else. And you have to link the distinctive features of your offering to the C-Level Insight and Core Imperative.

The distinctiveness of your offering is not limited to the features and functions of your product or service. It can stem from the way your product is implemented, the ease and swiftness with which you guide customers through your sales process, the mastery your customers attain with the support of your customer success team, or the expertise and experience your people bring, which far outmatch those found elsewhere in the market. Clearly articulate what makes your offering distinctive from everything else available.

Finding a Distinctive Value Proposition is certainly not a new concept. Countless sales books talk about finding and promoting what makes you different. The key for a Mega Dealer is the ability to link the distinctiveness of your value proposition to the attainment of the customer's Core Imperative using a C-Level Insight to tie it all together.

Now that the three components of a Mega Deal Premise have been discussed, the image on the next page shows how they work together.

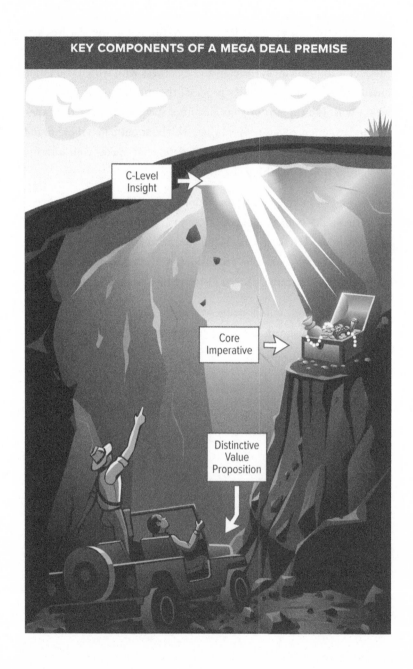

KEY COMPONENTS OF A MEGA DEAL PREMISE

C-Level Insight

Core Imperative

Distinctive Value Proposition

In this analogy, your customer's Core Imperative is the future state, the treasure they seek in their quest for improvement and where your solution can take them. The C-Level Insight is the revelation of the true nature of the problem, which brings to light why your Distinctive Value Proposition is the ideal vehicle to transport your customer on their journey of transformation. For Bob Iger, once he had set up the Core Imperative (we must fix Disney Animation) and the C-Level Insight (we are losing the innovation battle to Pixar), he was ready to deliver his Distinctive Value Proposition. He explained that he could only see three possible ways forward. First, they could leave the same management team in place and hope they would be able to turn Disney Animation around. But that didn't seem to be working. Second, they could try to find some new talent to hire. But he had been searching far and wide for six months and nobody was right for the job. Finally, they could buy Pixar. By pitching his solution this way, he framed Pixar as the one and only solution for turning around Disney Animation. They had to buy Pixar.

How to Craft a Mega Deal Premise

One of the most frequent questions my Mega Deal students ask me is "How do I come up with a compelling Mega Deal Premise?" My first response is "You shouldn't have to; your management team should provide it to you." However, after discussing this topic with hundreds of sellers, it is clear the vast majority of companies today tend not to have the internal capability to generate compelling, customer-specific insights for their sales teams.

So I've developed the recipe below.

It generally falls upon reps to craft an end-to-end Mega Deal Premise on their own. However, you'll be much more effective if you attempt this with a small team behind you. Before you start looking for your Mega Deal Premise, identify the best people from Presales, Product Strategy, and Marketing. Then ask yourself these questions:

- Who knows your solution the best?
- Who knows the competitive solutions the best?
- Who can work with your customer to measure and analyze their current problem and map out a solution using your offering?

Once you've located these three key people, you're ready to start crafting your Mega Deal Premise.

As mentioned earlier, discovering a customer's Core Imperative and developing a profound C-Level Insight and Distinctive Value Proposition that map to that Core Imperative isn't easy. In fact, it's what the big management consulting firms get paid millions for. They use proven frameworks to diagnose and solve the most critical challenges of large corporations. When you're looking for an insight as an enterprise seller, these same frameworks can be extremely helpful to you as well. The following step-by-step process for developing a C-Level Insight is partially based on the problem-solving model used by McKinsey & Company, which is arguably the most prestigious management consulting firm in the world.

1. COLLECT RELEVANT DATA

Much of your insight's potency lies in the credibility of the data you produce to back up any claims you make. In *The McKinsey Way*, Ethan M. Rasiel writes, "Facts are the bricks with which you will lay a path to your solution and build pillars to support it." As a seller you will generally be presenting your Mega Deal Premise to a customer stakeholder with many years of experience in a certain area of business. This is usually someone who has risen through the ranks and seen countless business scenarios unfold. Thus, they'll likely have strong gut instincts about the validity or falsity of any claims you make. Because you will often be significantly less experienced in their business than they are, the best way to ensure your insight will be taken seriously is to possess a deep and wide command of the facts.

When developing a Mega Deal Premise, there are four main categories where you and your team should focus to build your base of facts: your company, your competition, your customers, and your ecosystem.

Your Company

- **Mission:** What motivates your company and how is that unique in the market?
- **Business model:** What value do you offer the market, how do you deliver it, and how do you make money?
- **Product:** What are your off-the-shelf scalable offerings?
- **Services:** What tasks and outcomes do your people deliver?
- **Implementation:** How quickly and painlessly can you deliver value to your customers?
- **Customer success:** How do you enable your customers to reap measurable benefits from your offering over time?

Your Competition

- **Value propositions:** What are the central arguments your competitors make about why customers should do business with them?
- **Features and functions:** List and describe the functionality of all relevant competitive offerings. Which are unique and which are broadly available?
- **Market share:** How much of your market have your

competitors captured, both individually and collectively?

- **Customers:** List out the customers of each of your major competitors by size and industry (or other useful categories, like region, niche, etc.).
- **Selling style:** How do your competitors sell and when do they beat you? When do you win?

Your Customers

- **Ideal customer profile:** Who are the specific customer stakeholder types who buy from you? Why do they buy? What are they trying to achieve when they do?
- **Problem statement:** What problem does your offering solve *in the words of the customer?*
- **Use cases:** List specific examples of how customers have successfully used your solutions.
- **Alternative ways to solve the problem:** What other ways could the customer solve their problem or achieve their goal? What if the customer built their own system? Or hired low-cost resources in other countries?
- **Stakeholder experience:** What does a "day in the life" look like in the customer's current reality? Is the business process in question slower, more complex, or more costly than it should be? How does it impact worker bees, managers, and executives?
- **Business processes:** Map the entire end-to-end business process where your offering is relevant, as well as related upstream and downstream business processes.
- **Tech stack:** For tech companies, track your customer's technical environments to look for common configurations of technologies. Do prospects with a specific tech stack tend to buy your solution more often than others?

Your Ecosystem

- **Partners:** List all the players with whom you collaborate in terms of marketing, implementation, consulting, evaluation, monitoring, etc.
- **Tangential suppliers:** List all the suppliers who offer related or complementary solutions.
- **Other third parties:** List anyone else who is relevant in your niche, including market analysts, industry media, regulators, etc.

2. CREATE AN INITIAL HYPOTHESIS

For many sellers working to craft their first Mega Deal Premise, it's a struggle to know where to start. Take a stab at making a hypothesis based on your initial impressions and gut feeling. What does your experience (however limited it may be in the specific use case you are investigating) tell you about what an insight could be? You will test your hypothesis and iterate until you get it right, but start from an imperfect guess and progress from there.

One way to generate your first hypothesis is to lay out all the facts you currently know on paper or on a whiteboard. Look at the problem the customer is facing and at the value propositions of your main competitors. Focus on what is distinctive about what your company does or how you do it. Put a spotlight on that difference and use it as the trailhead of your journey to the customer's Core Imperative.

Saama Technologies Finds Their Distinctive Value Proposition

One of the companies I work with, Saama Technologies, provides analytics solutions. Very competitive market. There are several long-standing competitors with huge chunks of market share—Tableau, Qlik, Oracle, and many others. Through working with the Saama team we laid out the various flavors of value each company used in their go-to-market messaging. Just a few examples are below:

- **Tableau:** "Harness the power of your data"; "Tableau helps people see and understand data"
- **Qlik:** "Deliver real-time, active intelligence"; "Turn raw data into remarkable outcomes"
- **Oracle Analytics Cloud:** "Help people see data in new ways, discover insights, unlock endless possibilities"

We brainstormed on what made Saama's solutions different from those of their main competitors. We found that despite all the powerful analytics features, functions, and appealing user interface, the stand-out elements in Saama's products were their artificial intelligence (AI) capabilities natively built into each analytics package. The AI changed the way users interacted with the data, moving away from manually hunting for data points in dashboards and reports to literally asking the system, via voice, questions like "Are all our projects in Europe on track for on-time completion?" The system would produce the answer instantly.

Based on that differentiator, we developed the concept of intelligent analytics. We came up with stories and talk tracks like: "My vacuum cleaner runs itself. Pretty soon our cars will drive themselves. Our devices and applications are being built to be smart. Shouldn't your clinical applications be smart too?"

At the time I wrote this book, Saama had entered their hyper-growth phase by leading with their differentiated story about AI-driven analytics.

Next, analyze how your distinctive offering can address the customer's problem. To make sure you are always starting from facts, rather than hunches, ask yourself what the facts tell us about the following:

- The source of the problem
- The nature of the problem
- The alternative approaches to solve the problem
- Relationship between the problem and the Core Imperative
- Relationship between the problem and your Distinctive Value Proposition

3. TEST THE HYPOTHESIS

To really nail a customer-specific insight, you'll need to work with the customer and get under the hood to collect data so you can test your initial hypothesis. The best way to do this is to convince a customer to grant you access to internal people and data, a process known as collaborative investigation. If you can pull it off, you want to take measurements on the time, money, and resources that are currently being wasted. You might visit a call center and use a stopwatch to time how long it takes agents to find the right answers to callers' questions. You could hold workshops to get input from customer stakeholders about a specific business process. You may want to go on a ride-along so you can understand firsthand the experience of employees on the shop floor. Find ways to engage customers to root out all aspects of the problem you are working to solve.

The measurements themselves are very important. You want to quantify things like how long a process takes, how much money it costs, or how many people are involved. These metrics are the building blocks of a rock-solid understanding of the true nature of the problem. The reason to capture these measurements is not only to articulate the facts clearly but also to highlight how good or bad things really are. Between the facts your team collects internally and the evidence you are able to collect with the customer, you can achieve a much clearer understanding of the problem and how it might be addressed.

The next part of the puzzle is to map the cascade of impact. You want to be able to draw a clear connection between fixing this problem and impacting the Core Imperative. This could include multiple steps, and it often will. If the connection were obvious, the customer would have noticed it already. Your job is to hunt for something they aren't aware of yet.

When Bob Iger was looking to pitch the Pixar deal to his board, he collected two types of data. The problem he wanted to highlight was simply that Disney's recent movies weren't very good. And the Core Imperative was to be the most beloved media company among mothers of children under twelve years old. So he compiled the numbers for the last ten years to show that the studio had lost $400 million and almost none of the movies were critically acclaimed. Next, he conducted market research by surveying mothers of children under twelve to ask which movie studios they trusted the most. This proved bad movies were affecting their Core Imperative. It was a simple two-step map from the problem to the Core Imperative. A motivated sales rep can also obtain this kind of data about a company by digging into the financials of their recent projects and doing thorough discovery work with customer stakeholders or others in the ecosystem.

4. ITERATE

Sometimes your initial hypothesis will prove to be true, while other times it will fall flat. Often your solution will produce an incremental improvement but nothing close to a transformative capability. Whenever your results are anything less than superlative, take your learnings and try again. This might mean tweaking the hypothesis or developing an entirely new one.

This can be painstaking work, and it should always be a team effort spearheaded by Marketing, Product Strategy, and Presales. It's very difficult to craft a compelling Mega Deal Premise all by yourself.

5. TELL THE STORY

Once you have a proven insight, supported by data, it's time to make the facts tell a story. The story of a Mega Deal Premise begins with the customer's current state, highlighting their pains and inefficiencies. Next, you'll describe why this is the current reality. Speak in detail about what works and what doesn't work with regard to the current process, using facts and figures to support your story.

Then you'll offer a brighter alternative. Use a transition phrase like "What if things could be much better?" Next, lay out your C-Level Insight, which brings to light new information, never before heard by the customer. It could be data that disproves long-held beliefs about the source of the problem, or it could be a new innovation that, when applied, will solve the issue beyond all expectation.

Finally, reveal your Distinctive Value Proposition. This is when you'll bring your story to a climactic end by telling how the new information revealed in your insight can best be harnessed using your solution (versus any other alternative) to enable the customer to achieve their Core Imperative.

Some of the best stories describing a Mega Deal Premise are detailed and circuitous. They wind like a river from easy-to-understand images of workers at their desks struggling to finish a task to a behind-the-scenes interpretation of what is actually happening in the guts of the system. If the story was simple and straightforward, it wouldn't have remained a mystery for so long.

Within the story you should always include a discussion of how many ways the business challenge can be addressed and why your solution is the best or only way to achieve maximum results. This is what Bob Iger did when he walked through the three possible paths forward to fix Disney Animation and explained why two of the options didn't make sense. This left only one possible move: buy Pixar.

The story of your Mega Deal Premise must include facts at every step of the way, highlighted with credible numbers. Use measurements and percentages liberally to paint a believable picture of the sizable distance that can be crossed between the before-and-after scenarios by implementing your solution. The context and detail of the story should clearly show how your solution, better than any alternative, can cure a debilitating business pain or enable a transformational capability.

At its core, the story of your Mega Deal Premise is the tool you'll use to take your customers on a journey from their current state to the achievement of a Core Imperative. The hero of the story is your Distinctive Value Proposition, and the map leading the way is your C-Level Insight.

The Opportunity Comes Together

My detective work at the crash lab had gotten me closer to a C-Level Insight on the Enginex account; I now knew each missed regulatory deadline cost the company $10 million. But I still hadn't uncovered a captivating story about the hidden root of the problem.

"I need to understand something," I said, seated in a small conference room with Giovanni, Arun, and Victor. "Why are we coming so close to missing the deadlines?"

"Well," Arun said, bristling, "we've never missed one yet. And the delays aren't entirely our fault."

"All right." I backpedaled. "It's not a criticism, I'm just trying to understand the problem. Can you walk me through everything that happens after a request comes through from Enginex? Where does it go first?"

Victor leaned forward, interested. Giovanni stifled a yawn.

"The first stop," Arun explained, "is our dispatch board. The operators read the request, determine the type of analysis needed, and route the job to a team. Most Enginex requests are sent to our team in India. But sometimes they go to our Romanian team if India can't take them right away. Dubai gets a fair amount of Enginex work too."

"How long does that take?" Victor asked. "How many hours to get a team in place?"

Arun squirmed.

"Depends," he said. "If the first-choice team is ready and available they can be working in as little as six hours. But if not . . . anywhere from two to five days."

"And once the analysis begins," Victor pressed, "how long does it take?"

"Between four and six days," Arun replied. "If our team has questions for the customer, those are sent to the onshore services team, who relays them to Enginex and forwards the responses as soon as they come in. Time delays can slow things down by a day or two."

"Then what?" I asked. "How does the report get to Enginex when it's done?"

"Well," Arun said, "it follows the same route from the offshore analysts to the onshore services team. The time differences often cost us an extra day there too."

Victor, arms folded, holding his chin, was thinking hard.

"How close are we to missing the eight-day deadline?" Victor asked.

"We are coming very close lately," Arun said, embarrassed. "It's getting worse."

"With so many delays, how have we managed to meet the deadline so far?" I asked.

Arun stirred. "Our managers go crazy and pull out all the stops at the last minute to expedite. It's not sustainable."

Victor let out a low whistle and leaned back from the table.

"Giovanni," I asked, starting to get excited, "can you crunch some numbers for me? I think this is the insight we're looking for! How does our pricing for the analysts work on this contract?"

"We bill our analysts out at $100 per hour," he said.

"And how much would we have to charge," I pressed, "to hire a dedicated team for this customer? What if we had a team located right in their zip code that was sitting around waiting for the next job from Enginex? No dispatcher, no Dubai, no delays, just a group of people familiar with Enginex who are ready for anything they send?"

"That's not practical," Arun interjected. "The team would be free half the time. They would be paid to sit and wait for Enginex to send something. It could be a month at a time without any new work. Would you invoice Enginex for that downtime? How inefficient."

"I know it sounds crazy," I said. "But how much would it cost?"

Giovanni closed his eyes. He was computing. He held up a finger. We all sat in silence. Then he snapped back to reality.

"This team," he said, "would be billed out at $250 per hour, rather than $100. And because they would be on call every day regardless of workload, the services portion of the contract would increase by a factor of five. From five million to twenty-five million."

"And why would they ever agree to that?" Arun asked. "Why pay five times more to get something done a mere couple days faster? It doesn't make sense, Jamal. Corporate would never approve something like this. It's too far outside the scope of how we do things."

"Yes, I know," I said, excitedly, "but every missed deadline costs Enginex $10 million! And we're getting closer to missing one. At the current rate we're due to miss as many as *five* deadlines during the next contract cycle. That would cost them *$50 million*. Faster handling of the data is a Core Imperative for this account, and the C-Level Insight is that the location of the analysis team overseas is responsible for slowing down the process. Giovanni just told me a designated team would only increase the contract from $10 million to $30 million. They'd be paying us $20 million in order to save $50 million. *That's* our Distinctive Value Proposition!"

Giovanni's eyes widened. "Ten million per missed deadline?" he repeated, incredulous. "Is that . . . are you *sure* that number is correct?"

"It's true." Victor nodded. "I heard it myself. Enginex is financially accountable for hitting regulatory deadlines. If they miss one by even a day they have to pay a fine of $10 million."

"But could we get that construct approved?" I asked Victor. "It's against our policies to dedicate specific resources to just one customer, especially our best people."

Victor thought for a moment. Then he nodded.

"I'll make it happen."

*　　*　　*

To create the Mega Deal Premise for Enginex I involved numerous people from within my company, journeyed to the customer's site, and asked many difficult questions. It all started when Giovanni helped me identify a Core Imperative: handling intellectual property better was something Enginex cared about. Then, at the crash lab, I learned the real problem was the increasing threat of missing a deadline. But it wasn't until Arun explained our internal process that I was able to see the delays were occurring because our analysts were in multiple locations overseas and that team assignment and other delays could really put project timelines at risk. That was my insight. From there it was easy to craft a unique solution: build the customer a dedicated onshore team. Together, these elements made up a complete Mega Deal Premise.

Putting It All Together

The Mega Deal Premise is what you get when you combine a Core Imperative with a C-Level Insight and a Distinctive Value Proposition. The Premise is critical to every stage of a Mega Deal. It's a bright red thread, woven through the fabric of the deal from the beginning of your sales process to the end. It ties everything together. This single narrative will captivate senior stakeholders, justify the customer's investment of time and energy, and solidify your solution's valuation against challenges from procurement.

The first time you'll introduce your Mega Deal Premise to the customer is during the First Executive Meeting, which we'll cover in the next chapter. During that meeting you'll use the Premise to suggest conducting a limited test of your solution for the customer. The ultimate buying decision for your Mega Deal is going to be made based on the results of that test.

Case Study: Mark Coombs Crafts a Compelling Mega Deal Premise

When I met Mark Coombs he was a twenty-eight-year-old enterprise rep at a midstage tech company. We were introduced by his manager with whom I had worked as a field rep at a startup in Chicago in the early 2000s. Mark and I hit it off immediately, and he became my very first Mega Deal student.

Mark worked for a company that had been selling to the legal world for years. He and a few other reps were hired to expand their customer base beyond the legal market. Mark and I did a review of his accounts and settled on a global financial services company as his Mega Deal candidate account due to its size and the scope of potential usage of his product. If he could craft a compelling Mega Deal Premise, there was capacity within the account for a Mega Deal.

Step 1: Distinctive Value Proposition

Mark started by assessing what was differentiated or unique about his offering. He compared his product to his main competition and the customer's status quo. Based on internal discussions with his executive team and product team, and his knowledge of customer feedback in the field, Mark identified key points of distinction:

- Mark's product was the strongest at one key task: getting contractual information (most competitors in the area offered an *all-in-one solution* that could get information, store it, and create new versions of it).
- Mark's team could do a short and easy Proof of Concept (PoC) and implement the solution quickly.

- Mark could bring very senior executives from his company to engage with customer executives.
- Given the size of the opportunity and the company's desire to expand their addressable market beyond law firms, Mark's company was willing to commit to developing their product toward the candidate account's requirements.

Step 2: Core Imperative

To hone in on his account's Core Imperatives, Mark dove into their annual reports, listened to replays of analyst calls, and watched investor-day presentations. He spoke with a trusted system integrator partner who had worked with both the customer and his company, and he knew a lot of critical information regarding the customer's technical and political landscape. He also spoke with several middle managers within the account to gather information. His research yielded three Core Imperatives:

- Expand into EMEA and Asia.
- Grow top-line revenues 40 percent over three years through acquisitions.
- Build systems to manage data globally.

Step 3: C-Level Insight

Here is where things got interesting. Mark had sat in on many customer conversations during the previous year, and by comparing their responses, he realized the average cost to execute due diligence on all of the contracts for a new acquisition target was $10 million and it required three months of work. This is because the reviews were being outsourced to law firms who used teams of high-cost attorneys to manually review all of the acquisition target's contracts one at a time.

Mark's company was a pioneer in leveraging artificial intelligence (AI) technology to automate the review and analysis of documents. The insight they shared across all their customers was: "AI has reached a level of maturity where it can be leveraged to review and analyze corporate contracts many times faster than human lawyers, and at a fraction of the cost."

Mark further personalized that insight to fit the use case of his Mega Deal candidate account: "Using AI can cut the timeline and cost of contract review for a new acquisition target from three months and $10 million to one week and $90,000."

After completing my Mega Deal masterclass, Mark broke through to an Executive Vice President at one of the world's largest financial institutions. He set up a meeting with the EVP and went in prepared to deliver the story of his Mega Deal Premise.

The narrative he prepared went like this:

Mr. EVP, I've been studying your annual report, and I see you aim to grow topline revenue 40 percent by acquisition over the next three years. That's an ambitious goal given the current climate in your market. The obvious challenges are clear: identifying quality targets, estimating synergies with your core business, and assessing the present value of every target with precision. However, if you look deeper, there is another issue your mergers and acquisitions team is facing where the impact is much larger than you may be aware.

I recently spoke with your M&A team and heard how much contract due diligence review is costing them in time and money. Every acquisition target your company is considering has hundreds of thousands of active contracts. Those are outsourced to third-party experts for review. We know the average cost to review contracts for each acquisition target is approximately $10 million and it takes three months to complete.

If you extrapolate those numbers to the volume of acquisition targets you will need to analyze, acquire, and integrate into your core business, it's a real stretch to reach your CEO's goal to grow revenue 40 percent by acquisition. It will be cost prohibitive, and you'll never be able to acquire quality companies fast enough to hit that target. Contract review is the bottleneck. Reduce the time and cost of contract review and you can hit your goal.

Mark did some math on the whiteboard showing the return on investment for shifting the customer's current manual patent review to his AI solution. He also addressed the high-level costs and timelines of three other areas in the acquisition process the customer could tackle. His handwriting was terrible, but the message was clear as day. Mark's solution would complete three months' worth of contract reviews in a matter of hours (at a cost of $90,000 rather than $10 million). It turns out that the time savings was even more important than money to this EVP because he currently had a critical acquisition target he needed to close on in a few months.

The story for Mark's Mega Deal Premise linked the customer's Core Imperative to their Distinctive Value Proposition by revealing a C-Level Insight. This not only closed the deal, it exploded the contract to an astronomical level of impact. That EVP was also in charge of managing contracts for the company's core business. He immediately saw the value for an even wider use of the tool than Mark had suggested, and he asked his procurement department to negotiate a three-year enterprise deal with Mark's company.

This executive conversation won Mark the buy-in he needed to close the largest deal in his company's history. With this deal his company would have not only a marquee customer, but the resources to build out their offering for a new industry vertical. Mark's story is living proof that Mega Deals can change the course of companies.

Keep Your Eyes on the Summit

A Mega Deal Premise is hard to find, and you'll need significant knowledge about the customer's problems in order to locate one. Even though your vision as a Mega Dealer is to engage senior executives, a ton of prework needs to be done at the lower levels to uncover facts you will need to build your case.

In the case of Enginex Testing, I went to the crash lab looking for information. That's where Victor and I learned from a lab technician that missed deadlines cost Enginex $10 million each. Engaging with lower-level people opened the door for me to discover the C-Level Insight.

You don't set off to climb a mountain without scouting and planning your route. Spend some time camped out at the base of your Mega Deal mountain before you begin your ascent. Watch the weather conditions and talk to other climbers about their experiences. Use this time to gather data. You need to engage some workers at base camp before you take off for the summit.

But be careful. Spend too long at the bottom of the mountain and you'll become associated with that level of the organization. When you involve worker bees in your process, they start to feel ownership of the relationship with you. And this can lead to headaches down the road. It's best to keep lower-level employees at arms' length. Don't make commitments to them that keep you stuck at their level. Don't pitch them on your big ideas like they are your main contact. And definitely don't get single-threaded by engaging with only one of them. Meet with multiple worker bees, preferably in different reporting lines. Engage just enough to get some hard data, then focus on taking those learnings to more senior players.

If you "spill the candy in the lobby," and share too much with the lower players about your Mega Deal Premise, you'll open the door for them to tell you yes or no. But they don't have the authority for that. And they don't have the vision of an executive, so they aren't going to get on board with a transformational deal. Your idea is too big for these people to handle.

Start at the bottom, but keep your eyes on the summit.

With Enginex, I had to dig deep to learn what their Core Imperatives were. Turns out they had a regulatory compliance failure ten years previously where they missed a structural weakness on a new windshield design. The mistake led to hundreds of injuries and two deaths over the span of three years. When regulators discovered the fault was with Enginex's testing, they fined the company 5 percent of their revenue during the three-year period. Enginex took sweeping action to revamp their quality control and made regulatory compliance an ongoing C-level priority. Today, they are a poster child for auto safety.

Given that background, *any* regulatory gap is taken seriously. Once I discovered this Core Imperative, I was ready to tie in a C-Level Insight. That emerged during my talk with Arun, when I learned that the time difference between our dispatch board and offshore analysis team was driving the delays. Finally, I had to develop a Distinctive Value Proposition. I did that when I found a unique way to fix Enginex's problem: a designated team of onshore analysts.

Once I had my Mega Deal Premise laid out, it was time to convey this information to one of Enginex's top executives and get his approval to run a Proof of Concept study to test my idea.

It was time for the First Executive Meeting.

CHAPTER SUMMARY

An ideal Mega Deal candidate account is a company with a burning desire to fix a problem and significant budget to invest in a solution. Leverage your own executives or board members to make the connection, or reach out to partners to gain an introduction.

A **Mega Deal Premise** is an insightful or nonobvious way for a customer to achieve their deepest desires by using your product. It includes three crucial components:

- **Core Imperative:** One of your customer's most important goals, set by senior management
- **C-Level Insight:** A new discovery or way of thinking about what stands between the customer's current state and the achievement of one of their Core Imperatives
- **Distinctive Value Proposition:** A clear story demonstrating how your offering is the best or only solution to help the customer remove the pain and achieve their goal

The combination of a Core Imperative, C-Level Insight, and Distinctive Value Proposition is critical to every stage of a Mega Deal. This single narrative will captivate senior stakeholders, justify the customer's investment of time to validate your claim, establish the price tag you will put on your solution, and help you defend against challenges from procurement.

CHAPTER 2

THE FIRST EXECUTIVE MEETING

I was flipping through my slides one more time, practicing what I was going to say, when the office door swung open and Bill McClellan popped out. He was jabbering into a pair of AirPods, a trendy leather knapsack slung casually over one shoulder. Bill was cooler than I'd imagined. For some reason, I figured he'd look nerdy and out of shape. But the man walking toward me was a rock star.

As he strolled past, Bill waved at me to follow him. Then he was out the door and climbing into the elevator. I jumped up and raced after him.

"Those financial projections sound questionable," he was saying as I bounced into the elevator. "Did you already build a 10 percent margin into that? And what if we can't renew for the same rate at two years? I'd say it's fifty-fifty." Bill winked at me and pressed the button for the executive parking garage.

Next thing I knew we were climbing into a silver Lamborghini Performante and Bill was still on the phone. The vibrations ripped through my chest as he fired up the engine and tore out of the garage. I was thrown back into my seat as Bill merged onto the freeway and pushed the needle past 100 miles per hour.

By the time Bill finally hung up his call, we were nearly at Enginex and I was very close to vomiting. Bill handled the Lambo like a race-car driver, swerving through traffic, slamming on the brakes, and accelerating past other motorists like they were standing still. He seemed to approach life like one big video game.

"Sorry about that," he shouted over the thundering engine as he hung up the phone. "How's it going, Jamal? What's up? What am I doing in this meeting? Just trying to charm the guy, right? You want some gum?"

I was completely thrown off. My heart was racing. We were less than two minutes from Enginex, and there was no way I could get through my carefully practiced presentation. I shook my head at the pack of Juicy Fruit he was holding out. He shrugged, shoving three sticks into his mouth.

"We need you to pitch Lars on a new way of structuring their analysis team," I started. "See, right now they are using our standard bench at $100 per hour. But we're getting dangerously close to missing a deadline. We have this idea that we could build their team a different way."

Bill turned up the front drive of Enginex headquarters. He was barely listening to me.

"Sure." He nodded, checking his hair in the rearview mirror. "We'll make them a better team. Got it."

"Yes," I stammered, "but that's only part of the—" We pulled up to the security checkpoint, and Bill leaned out of his window, smiling at the woman in the booth.

"Hey there." He oozed charm. "I think it's so admirable, everything you folks do to keep us all safe. I salute you."

She blushed. I rolled my eyes. Was this guy for real? He was wasting our precious preparation time, and he seemed completely oblivious. Or maybe he just didn't care. I glanced at my watch. The big meeting started in five minutes.

"It's not so bad," she said, holding up a self-help book. "I get to read a lot."

"Wow." Bill shook his head. "I'd be on Insta all day myself."

The woman laughed and waved for Bill to hurry up. A line of cars was forming behind us. He said we were meeting with Lars Reinhoff, and she raised her eyebrows. Then she printed us a pass for the dashboard, wished us luck, and told Bill to let her know how it went on the way out. He winked and pulled forward.

As Bill and I walked up the steps to the reception area, I gave him last-minute instructions.

"Remember," I said, "stress the finality of the May 31 deadline. We can't have this deal slip into next fiscal."

"Yeah, yeah." He waved a hand at me. "Sure, I got it. I'll let you know how it goes." And with that, he turned away from me and headed into the lobby alone.

"Wait!" I jumped after him. "What are you doing? I'm coming with you."

Again, Bill waved his hand at me.

"Naw." He shook his head. "This is something I need to do alone. You can wait in the car if you want."

He tossed me his keys. I hadn't expected this. Was Bill trying to steal this customer? Was he just arrogant and didn't think he needed help? I couldn't figure out why he was resisting me, but I didn't have time to think about it. This was *my* meeting, and *my* customer, and *my* ass on the line if I couldn't get this deal done. There was no way I was letting Bill McClellan shove me out.

"Whoa, whoa, whoa," I said, chasing after him. "Listen, that guy is going to say a lot of stuff you don't understand or care about. But every detail is critical for getting the deal done and keeping the relationship in place. I need to be present so I can make sure to follow up and execute on everything you discuss."

Bill sighed and shook his head. Then he turned, without a word, and strolled past me. I froze, unsure what to do. Then a feeling of defiance exploded inside me. *Screw this*, I thought to myself. *I will NOT be cut out of my own deal.*

I took a deep breath and made my decision: I was heading in on Bill's heels.

*   *   *

Meeting with an EVP at Enginex was the only way I could obtain approval for the kind of revolutionary deal I had in mind. But senior executives aren't easy people to get appointments with. That's why I'd asked one of my company's own EVPs, Bill McClellan, to set up a meeting with my target at Enginex: an EVP named Lars Reinhoff. With a single phone call Bill was able to get on Lars's calendar—something that would have required months of maneuvering without his help. The only thing I didn't anticipate was how difficult it would be to get Bill to focus and take the meeting seriously.

Why Hike When You Can Fly?

After you've identified your candidate account and worked out your Mega Deal Premise, it's time to go straight to the top of the business unit you are looking to sell into. That means meeting directly with a senior executive. For many reps, this is counterintuitive, if not fear-provoking. Executives are hard to reach. For these busy people, talking with sales reps is a low priority—or something to avoid altogether. They train their assistants and security staff to keep sales reps away. As a result, most sellers don't even try to get in front of executives early in a sales cycle.

A Run-Rate Selling mentality is built on the assumption that a seller must start at the bottom of the customer's organization and slowly work their way up the various levels of management using calls, demos, presentations, and introductions until the rep finally reaches senior stakeholders with the right combination of influence, decision-making power, and budget. As widely held as this selling perspective may be, it is not the way of the Mega Dealer.

The difference between the Run-Rate Selling mentality and the Mega Dealer mindset is similar to the difference between a mountain climber and a heli-skier.

A mountain climber's goal is to make it from base camp to the top of the mountain through personal effort, hard work, and endurance. It might take days or weeks to get there, and the climber will have to avoid danger at every step on the way to the summit. Then, after arriving, it's time to turn around and begin the arduous task of trekking back down the mountain.

If you are going to chase and land a transformative deal, you need to stop mountain climbing. Working your way up from low-level contacts to executives is time-consuming and presents obstacles that can slow or even prevent you from ever reaching the summit. There are blockers, bottlenecks, and dead ends every step of the way. To land a Mega Deal within your own lifetime, learn how to heli-ski.

A heli-skier's goal is to ski down the world's most epic mountains at top speed, leaping over outcroppings, slaloming right and left, and having the time of their life. To get to the top of the mountain a heli-skier takes a helicopter. **The summit isn't the final destination, it's the starting point.** It's where the fun begins, and a heli-skier wants to get there *fast*.

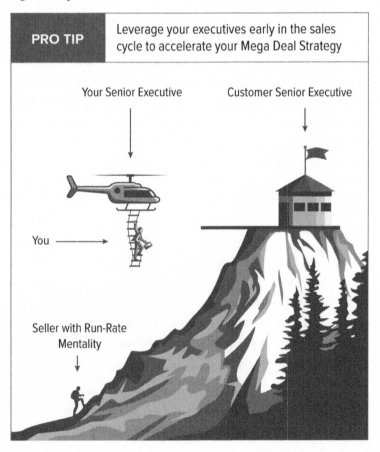

To become a heli-skier in enterprise sales, you'll need a helicopter. And your best shot at snagging a chopper ride is with your executives.

There are several reasons leveraging your own executives is such a powerful way to accelerate big deals. The biggest reason is that when you engage the right internal executive, they already have Peer Business Status with the customer executive you are trying to reach. This means both parties are on the same level in terms of perceived corporate stature, expertise, and business value.

One definition of Peer Business Status is based on title matching. In most business cultures, significant attention is given to where one sits in the management hierarchy. For instance, a few years ago I was with one of my EVPs and some executives from another Fortune 100 company playing golf. I'm not a golfer, so I was driving the cart. At one point I turned to the EVP and said, "I'm going to need executive involvement in a big deal at some point. When would you be open to coming in and saying a few words?"

He looked at me curiously as if the answer should be obvious. "When you have an EVP for me to talk to, call me," he replied. "If you've got a SVP, bring in Jack. He's my SVP." I couldn't help but smile. He didn't want to talk to anyone below him in terms of title. He was a title matcher.

For others, Peer Business Status is extended to those who exhibit knowledge or expertise around a specific business topic. I came to realize this on the Enginex deal when Giovanni and Arun suggested we bring in internal experts at various stages of the sales cycle. Although these people typically had titles like Manager or Director, it was clear when they spoke on their areas of expertise that they held Peer Business Status in the eyes of the customer VPs who attended those meetings.

This realization proved to me that even a lowly sales rep like me could achieve Peer Business Status with executives much more senior to me in terms of title and experience. I just had to know my stuff and be confident in how I positioned my assertions.

The reason Mega Dealers make a beeline to senior stakeholders right from the outset is that executives make Mega Deals happen. I've never seen a significant deal that didn't include executive involvement, influence, and approval. Executives hold the cards when it comes to game-changing transactions. They have broad influence over buying decisions—and sometimes outright decision-making power and authority over the budget. They are also highly motivated to take action to improve the business because they're personally accountable for the well-being of a business unit, process, or outcome within the company.

The bigger a deal gets, or the more impactful a project becomes, the higher up the chain you'll have to go to get buy-in and sponsorship. The exact executive approval structure varies from one company to another, but a decent example would be when a deal that requires less than $500,000 in funding is often within the approval limits of a Vice President. When the budget hits the $1 to $5 million range, it's likely there will be a steering committee for the project with significant input from procurement. Move up to $10 million and the steering committee will have oversight from a Senior Vice President. At $20 million, the CFO gets involved. And at $50 million, you'll likely need the signature of an Executive Vice President or the CEO.

At the end of the day, the summit of your mountain is a meeting with the executive(s) accountable for achieving the Core Imperative your solution can address.

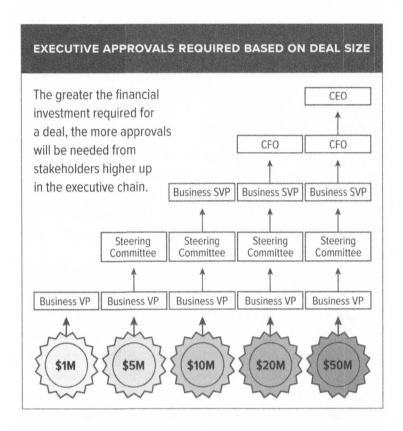

EXECUTIVE APPROVALS REQUIRED BASED ON DEAL SIZE

The greater the financial investment required for a deal, the more approvals will be needed from stakeholders higher up in the executive chain.

Bob Iger was the CEO, and he pitched the Pixar deal directly to his board of directors. Then he immediately got Steve Jobs on the phone, with whom he had Peer Business Status. That's how he was able to close a $7.4 billion deal start to finish in under six months.

I was able to convince Bill McClellan, our regional EVP, to attend the meeting with Lars because he was at Lars's level in terms of title and I knew he would look good if his region closed a massive deal. So I dangled the deal in front of him, asked him to set up a thirty-minute meeting, and promised to handle all of the preparation myself. I also knew Gunther would look good to Lars if he facilitated a meeting with an EVP from a major company, so I was able to get his help making the meeting happen. I landed myself in that room by helping these three executives all get something they wanted.

Executive Whispering

If there is one universal skill I have seen across all successful Mega Dealers, it is Executive Whispering, or the art of working with executives on both sides of the table. Working with executives is tricky business, and what may be counterintuitive is that often it is *our own* executives who are most difficult to work with. Many executives will say, "Get me involved in deals early." However, sellers are hesitant to bring them in at the beginning stages of a sales cycle, fearing that if they tap an executive to help out before a deal is fully qualified they'll risk getting blasted for wasting the executive's time if the engagement ends up falling through. Senior management often views reps who bring in opportunities that aren't fully baked and ready for signatures as sloppy or lazy. This attitude is common in the corporate world. In this environment, what sane rep is going to stick her neck out by bringing an executive into a potential deal before it's in the bag?

The problem with this mentality is that the early participation of supplier-side executives can greatly accelerate connection, interest, engagement, and resource allocation among customer executives. A small investment of your executive's time can motivate top brass on the customer side to conduct a serious investigation into the merits of your solution. It can be the ultimate way to qualify a Mega Deal. A few hours of engagement from one of your executives can shave months of arduous work off your mountain-climber ascent and confirm whether there is even *interest* in your value proposition from the executive who would ultimately sign the deal.

Executive Whispering is one of the biggest secrets for accelerating and winning Mega Deals.

Put yourself in the shoes of a busy senior executive and imagine you just received two requests for unsolicited pitch meetings. First, you got an email from me, Jamal Reimer, the sales rep. Then, before you could respond, you also got an email from Larry Page at Google, who wants to chat with you about a new opportunity. Who are you going to call back? Larry has authority, celebrity, and peer status within the social hierarchy of the executive world. He'll get the call back every time.

Your executives might not be Larry Page, but they are still a world apart from sales reps. Executives enjoy connecting with other executives. Sales reps are a big step down (or five steps down) from EVPs. That's why most of your meeting requests are ignored, refused, or deleted. Use Executive Whispering to ride your executives' coattails into impossible meetings instead.

Another way to hitch a helicopter ride into a meeting with customer executives is through partners. If you can find a consulting firm that has worked with both your company and your Mega Deal target, that can be a perfect way to gain an introduction directly to an executive.

This isn't about recruiting your executives or partners to do your job for you. Make it clear you'll be doing the legwork to actually schedule and plan the meeting. All the executive will have to do is show up and deliver the high-level messaging you lay out for them. This should be an attractive offer to your partners and executives. They will be excited about the chance to connect with other people who have similar status to them. It's like a cameo appearance in a movie.

The graphic below shows how much work the rep does behind the scenes to set up the few but highly impactful activities her executive carries out.

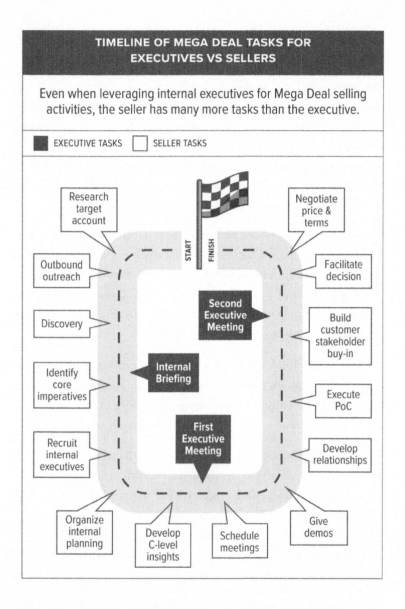

TIMELINE OF MEGA DEAL TASKS FOR EXECUTIVES VS SELLERS

Even when leveraging internal executives for Mega Deal selling activities, the seller has many more tasks than the executive.

■ EXECUTIVE TASKS □ SELLER TASKS

Research target account

Outbound outreach

Discovery

Identify core imperatives

Recruit internal executives

Organize internal planning

Develop C-level insights

Schedule meetings

Give demos

START FINISH

Second Executive Meeting

Internal Briefing

First Executive Meeting

Negotiate price & terms

Facilitate decision

Build customer stakeholder buy-in

Execute PoC

Develop relationships

When you engage in Executive Whispering you won't feel the pressure of engaging with senior customer executives on your own. Instead, you'll enlist the participation of your executives to level the playing field in terms of establishing Peer Business Status and accelerating talks between your organizations.

On the Enginex deal, once I recognized Lars Reinhoff as the summit of my mountain, I identified the corresponding person in my own company: Bill McClellan. Both he and Lars were EVPs. Also, Giovanni and Arun confirmed Bill was great with customers.

If your internal executives don't have great people skills, it can be a problem. I've seen senior executives spoil meetings when the chemistry with the customer wasn't there. Choose your executives and partners wisely. Do what you can to make sure there is a good fit.

When you're trying to determine the right executives and partners to attach to your deal, don't default to targeting the biggest big shot at your company. I've worked at companies where I would *never* take the top two or three executives into customer meetings. They just weren't good with customers. It's more important to find people who will take your deal seriously, who will be excited about getting involved, and who are empathetic leaders focused on the customer's reality, not their own agenda. Once you have a short list of names, ask around to find out which of your potential options is known for being good with customers and being willing to take direction from sales reps. Also, avoid anyone with a reputation for micromanaging. You want their help, but you don't want them to try to take over your deal.

If you get an executive or partner who isn't working out well, simply stop sending them updates about your deal and they will usually forget about it. If you have someone who sinks their teeth in and won't let go, you might have to get other members of management involved to back them off. Make sure you frame the conversation in terms of what is best for the customer. Tell your management chain why a certain executive or partner isn't a good fit and ask for their help getting the person to let go.

Once you've identified the right executive or partner to accompany you to meet with the customer's executive, you need to get your executive excited about your deal. You have to sell them on the level of pain the customer is going through, how well your solution can solve the problem, and the potential size of the deal. Executives and partners are busy, and attending a meeting with you and the customer can feel like a big ask to them. This is especially true if you work at a larger company with thousands of employees. Showing how you really have a shot at a Mega Deal will quickly get them excited and focused on helping you succeed.

One way to gain executive support is to talk at the right level. When you have the opportunity to speak with an executive about getting involved in your deal, keep your presentation tight and focus on the big picture. Give enough detail to be thorough, but don't get lost in the weeds unless senior people ask specific questions. Speak like executives speak to each other and they will see you more like a peer and less like a subordinate. This will help you get them interested in you and your deal.

Another way to gain support and favor from executives and partners is to **become an asset to them, professionally and personally**. As President John F. Kennedy said, "Ask not what your country can do for you. Ask what you can do for your country." Typical salespeople focus on themselves, and on what their executives can do for *them*. But Mega Dealers focus on serving their executives and providing value. They want to be people executives rely on.

I have an executive who's good at her job, but not recognized outside our company. When an industry conference asked me for keynote speaker recommendations, I threw her name in the hat. I'd seen her speak before, so I knew she'd be great. They invited her to speak and took professional photos of her in advance for promotional purposes. She still uses one of those photos on LinkedIn to this day.

Another time, there was a Danish executive I kept reaching out to and asking what we could do for him, but I wasn't hearing back. Then I learned our European office was hosting an event at the American Ambassador's residence in Copenhagen, which is a famous historical building that's otherwise off-limits to the general public. The estate was seized by the Nazis during WWII, and it was where they housed their most senior leaders in the region. After US forces drove out the Nazis, Denmark let the United States use the manor as its Ambassador's residence.

I called this executive and left a voicemail letting him know we had this event and I could get him in if he wanted to go. Ten minutes later he called me back and said he was in.

Any time you can do something for an executive or partner that enhances their status, you'll win points. Everyone likes to feel important. Find ways to be an asset to the executives and partners you work with and they will quickly develop a favorable impression of you and your Mega Deal.

The more you focus on becoming an asset, the less you'll be viewed as a "salesperson." Get out of the sales lane and more executives will want to be involved with your deals. There are many preconceived ideas about what it means to be a salesperson. Nobody looks forward to spending an hour on the phone with a salesperson. Wording and titles matter. Stereotypes about salespeople will hold you back from connecting with executives and partners in a meaningful way, so avoid associating yourself with this label.

If your job title includes "sales," change it to something more helpful and knowledgeable, like Account Manager. Get rid of the *S* word if you want to network with executives and senior-level partners.

The Meeting of My Career

I was devastated to be walking into the biggest meeting of my life unprepared, chasing after Bill like an unwanted sidekick. But before I could catch my breath, we were ushered into a conference room and found ourselves face-to-face with Lars Reinhoff. Bill didn't miss a beat. He strode around the table and met the Enginex EVP with a winning smile and firm handshake.

"Lars," he crooned, "I've been so looking forward to meeting you ever since I heard how you turned Tarka around in eighteen months. You're a legend in our neck of the woods. And was that your '63 Stingray in the garage? That ride is pristine, Lars. *Pristine.*"

Reinhoff broke into a boyish grin.

"Isn't she something?" he asked, looking at Bill like a dear old friend. "Found that car in Tokyo of all places. CEO of one of our suppliers had it squirreled away in his personal collection, the son of a gun." He rubbed the back of his neck. "You think a guy who wanted to keep a big customer happy would have given me a break, but we spent two months negotiating that deal."

"Son of a gun," Bill repeated, shaking his head.

The two men ignored me completely. I marveled at the immediate rapport and camaraderie they'd fallen into. There was no way I could have reached this level of connection with an EVP on my own. Despite his quirks, Bill was a huge asset. With him as my "sponsor," I'd vaulted over walls typical sellers spend months struggling to climb.

For ten minutes straight, the two men chatted animatedly about cars, stress, politics, business, handling "big-shot CEOs," and a spate of unrelated topics. At one point, Lars stuck his head out of the conference room to order some snacks and espresso. Bill flipped through a few photos of his own car collection. I started to wonder if I was going to get a chance to speak at all.

Then, suddenly, Bill turned to me and said, "Hey, this here's Jamal Reiner." (Actually, it's Reimer.) "This whole thing was his idea. He's your Account Manager, and he's one of our absolute top people." (Actually, I was average.) "He's got some phenomenal ideas about our engagement with you guys. Maybe we can shut up and listen for a minute while I chow down on these amazing éclairs."

Lars regarded me as if he was seeing me for the first time.

"Yes." He smiled at me. "Splendid."

And just like that I had the floor. I'd been given an open invitation from one of Enginex's top executives to pitch my Mega Deal opportunity. And he was listening attentively.

Adrenaline surged through my body, and I felt my fingers go numb and my chest start to tingle.

I was on.

Thankfully, I'd spent many hours preparing for this moment. Well, actually, I'd been preparing to train Bill for this moment. But since that whole situation was shot, I was about to drop the pitch myself. I had the strange sensation that my entire career had been leading up to this single moment. In the next three minutes, I was either going to get an invite to the big dance or be turned into a pumpkin.

"Mr. Reinhoff," I started, "I was at your crash lab last week and I learned that if we are late with one of our reports and your company misses a regulatory deadline Enginex will be fined $10 million by the regulators. We have not been late once yet. But upon deeper review, we have seen that latency in both our processes and yours are driving us collectively toward a high likelihood of *repeat* late deliveries."

Lars raised his eyebrow. "That," he said slowly, "is not good." He was working hard to keep his voice calm after hearing me predict a train wreck in his own shop. "Say more," he urged, "I need the detail."

"So I've been doing some digging," I said. "Speed is one of the main benefits of our software. Because we use predictive AI to build and run our statistical models on a state-of-the-art supercomputer, it's the fastest in the industry by a factor of two. So that's the good news." I walked over to the whiteboard, grabbed a marker, and started drawing boxes and arrows to illustrate the situation. "However, the services portion of the process is slowing everything down. Every time a request comes through from Enginex, it can take up to three days to put together a qualified team of analysts and bring them up to speed. Also, our analysts are located overseas, and we lose precious hours on every job due to time differences. Any questions have to be relayed from our offshore team to our onshore team and then forwarded to the right person within Enginex. That can take twelve hours per request, slowing things down even further."

Lars nodded, watching me intently as I spoke. He hadn't touched his pastry.

"I know your margins aren't great on these crash tests," I continued, trying to nail a pain point, "and that $10 million cuts directly into your bottom line. So we came up with a plan to eliminate the problems. We want to build you a dedicated team of our top analysts and house them onshore, right here in our city. They would be waiting for each new request from Enginex, ready to go at a moment's notice. And they would be in the same time zone, so no hours would be lost.

"Our projection is we could reduce the chances of a missed deadline by 75 percent—that would save you an expected exposure to $40 to $60 million on the next contract. However, we've never done it on this level with such tight deadlines, so we'd like to start with a small test, free of charge, on your next crash test. I've got this approved internally on our side. We want to go ahead and temporarily give you a designated team and host them at our offices here completely at our own cost. This way we can put your next crash test through both the standard process and the custom process in parallel and monitor the differences. You'll get a designated team for free, and we'll get all the data we need to confidently offer you this major service upgrade on your next contract."

The men were silent for a moment. Lars was thinking. Bill was obviously impressed at my preparation. He looked at Lars and shrugged, as if to say, *why not?*

"All right," Lars said after another minute. "Let's do it. What do you need from me?"

"First," I said, "can you confirm my numbers? Is it true that the fine is $10 million even when the deadline is missed by a single day?"

"Yep." Lars nodded. "I'm afraid so."

"And would a 50 percent reduction in the odds of a missed deadline be meaningful?" I asked. "Would that make a difference in the profitability of your division?"

"Without a doubt," he confirmed. "Mitigating risk is one of my main objectives this year. And that comes straight from Andre, our CFO. This would be massive."

"Then we are ready and willing to move forward on this," I said. "The only other things I need are an introduction to the right people on your team and access to your current data. And last, I ask that you agree to get back together with Bill and me in a couple months to look over the results of the test. If it all checks out like we think, the deadline to implement it is the end of the fiscal year on May 31—about six months from now. That's when your current contract renews and we'll have to get a new one in place by then."

"Sure," said Lars, "that all sounds fair. I'm happy to meet again in a couple months and end-of-year is a reasonable deadline for this. I'll let Gunther know it's OK to share the data you need. Keep me informed on how the test is coming in the meantime, and I look forward to hearing the results."

Ten minutes later, Bill and I were strolling through the parking garage back to his car and I was pumped. It had been one of the strangest meetings I'd ever witnessed, but somehow it delivered exactly the results I was looking for.

We walked by a sky blue–colored vintage sports car with white seats in a parking space labeled Reserved for Lars Reinhoff. I marveled at the fact that Bill had noticed the small sign on the way in and was able to use that knowledge to build rapport so effortlessly. The morning felt like a blur in my memory.

I wondered if the ride home was going to be awkward. Would Bill be angry with me for forcing my way into the meeting? However, he never mentioned it.

We hopped into the car, and Bill tossed his wallet and phone into a side compartment and put on his sunglasses.

"All right." He beamed, pointing the race car back toward our offices and zipping off. "I'm starving. You hungry? Man, I can't get over that '63 Stingray. Absolutely pristine. Want to grab a sandwich? I know a great spot."

*   *   *

My first meeting with Lars and Bill lasted just thirty minutes, but my team and I spent hundreds of hours preparing for it. I won Bill's interest, discovered the insight, crafted the Mega Deal Premise, and memorized the pitch. The reason for all the work was to secure three microcommitments from Lars. Together, those commitments opened a path to a Mega Deal.

The Three Microcommitments

Microcommitments are a series of relatively small commitments that establish increasing momentum toward a larger commitment. During the First Executive Meeting, focus your executive on obtaining three key microcommitments. First, get agreement to run a small assessment of your solution. Second, get the customer executive to agree they will attend, along with your executive, a meeting at the end of the assessment to review the results. Third, agree you will be given access to their current and past data specific to the use case to be used in the assessment.

As a Mega Dealer you have to shift the customer executive from their current vision, which doesn't include you or your product, to a new vision in which your company can solve their biggest problem and help them achieve their wildest dreams. That's a big change. And executives are a skeptical and slow-moving bunch. They aren't looking to take big risks because they are held responsible if things go south.

This is why your target executive needs to be wholly convinced your solution will work.

The best way to create a big change in someone's mentality is gradually—one step at a time. Instead of asking them to make a big decision all at once, create a series of tiny decisions that will lead them to the big decision slowly.

These three microcommitments are key to earning yourself all the runway you will need to prove the value your solution can bring as well as to secure an executive audience to hear the results and understand the potential impact your solution could bring to their organization.

It is super important that you impress upon your executive that the entire purpose of the First Executive Meeting is to achieve these three microcommitments. Without them your timeline to closure will increase or the deal will be much smaller or you may not get a deal at all.

You'll usually have just a very short window to get your higher-up ready for the First Executive Meeting. When I prepped Bill for our meeting with Lars, I never had his full attention. Talk with your executive before the meeting, but don't expect them to invest too much effort in the process. Stick with giving them these three very simple objectives.

Because executives are busy and distracted, it's a good idea to make an agenda for the First Executive Meeting and share it with your executive well in advance. Then try to coax your executive to get on calls prior to the meeting. You can also ride with your executive to the meeting and prepare them in the car on the way over. It's your job to make sure your executive is ready. Some executives resist this type of preparation because they feel they are experienced, know the drill, and would rather wing it. Plus, they aren't as invested in the deal as you and don't like being told what to do. This means you'll need to stay strong and stand your ground with your executive. If you let your executive walk into the meeting unprepared, the only person who suffers is you.

Executives tend to be high-level thinkers. They don't want to talk through the boring details and intricacies of technology or service engagements. They want the big picture. Tell your executive what your grand vision is for this account, and keep it concise. Don't overload these people with details. Don't get down in the weeds. Finally, repeat the goals for the first meeting.

The goals of the First Executive Meeting are to secure three micro-commitments from the customer executive:

1. Agreement to do an assessment

    Performing a collaborative assessment of your solution is a critical step in the Mega Deal process. This must be completed before you begin talking about the size and scope of any potential engagement. If you can prove to the customer that your solution will bring outsize benefits to their organization, you can build a compelling reason for them to agree to a deal of enormous size.

    The assessment could be a technical sandbox environment exercise, a Proof of Concept, or a pilot implementation. Explain to the executive that you've done similar programs for other customers, but you've never implemented this exact use case before. For this reason, you'd like to run a test. The assessment can be a paid exercise or free, depending on how your company works.

2. Agreement to meet again for the assessment results

    Executives are famous for losing interest in sales cycles or getting distracted by other priorities just when you need them most. Lock in executive attention from the outset by asking the customer executive, in the first meeting, to commit to attending a second meeting to hear the results of the assessment. This way the customer executive will hear directly from you, and not through subordinates, the outcomes your solution can bring and how much value can be unlocked by doing a deal with you.

The goal of this step is that the two executives need to look each other in the eye and agree to meet again. They are unlikely to blow off an industry peer after promising to meet.

3. Agreement to deliver current-state data

The results of your assessment will demonstrate the measurable business impact your solution can provide. However, unless these results are compared side by side against your customer's current numbers, you'll never know exactly how much value your solution provides. Middle management often seeks to hide current-state measurements from sales reps because they are afraid this data will expose their weaknesses to their own management. Without knowing how slow, complex, or inefficient their current reality is, it will be difficult to quantify how your offer improves the situation. I've been in many sales cycles where we didn't get that data up front and weren't able to provide evidence of massive value. In those cases, we went on to sell the solution for less than the price we were asking. Don't let this happen to you. Get the as-is metrics up front.

Thus, it is critical to obtain agreement up front from the customer executive that you and your team will be given access to their current-state data.

And here's a huge point that looks like a small detail— when the executive agrees to share their as-is data with you, be sure to get the name of the person you should follow up with for the numbers. Write down the name. Sorry for getting into the minutiae here, but without a specific person the executive assigns to this task, and given the sensitive nature of sharing internal performance data, once you try to actually get the data delivered, you will likely be tossed from person to person and spin your wheels for weeks. Get a clear line of sight to obtaining the data during the executive meeting.

Don't Talk Big Numbers

There is nothing that will strip your credibility faster than positioning a large deal before value is proven. In the first meeting, don't mention any dollar figures. Don't talk about contracts or terms. It's too soon. That's like talking about marriage on the first date. Instead, paint a compelling vision of the future. But don't go into detail about deal specifics just yet.

Take it one step at a time.

If an executive asks questions at this point that would lead into a commercial conversation, pump the brakes. It's too early to guess at how the financials might work out. If they ask how the arrangement would look, what the project might cost, how long the contract would last, or anything about the specifics of the deal, the best response is to cite customer success stories in terms of investment and positive return.

One way to answer questions about the size or the cost is to frame your response in terms of magnitude. For instance, you could say, "It's up to you whether you want to make this a big project or a small one and how you want to set it up, but right now the data suggests that for every dollar you put into it, you'll get a dollar fifty out in nine months.

The only way to be sure is to conduct a small assessment to get real numbers specific to your case."

Shift the focus from the deal to the microcommitments. Just get the three microcommitments and you will have won the day. Don't try to do any more than that during this meeting, even if things are going really well. Resist the urge to push it further.

Big decisions are hard to make. They require a lot of thinking, weighing options, and asking other people for opinions. But small decisions are easy. They seem obvious. You barely even have to consider those.

Your customers are the same way. Your job is to gradually lead them along a path to your deal one easy decision at a time. Getting the customer's executive to make microcommitments in the First Executive Meeting is not only doable, it's also a huge amount of progress for a single meeting.

Bring an Expert Wingman

Sometimes it makes sense to include your go-to subject matter expert in the First Executive Meeting, someone with credibility who knows how to dive into the details without getting lost in the weeds. It could be someone like a senior person from Product Management, an Engagement Consultant, or a Senior Presales Engineer. Having this person with you takes the pressure off your executive. The executive can relax and doesn't have to remember complicated details. Prepare the executive with a profound but simple talk track. All they have to do is act charming and deliver the headline, big idea, or exciting part of the story. Then the second player can jump in to give more detail and fill out the story. Also, when the customer starts asking hard questions, the second player will be right there with answers.

In the next chapter, I'll show you how to do a PoC. You'll see how to find the numbers needed to seal the Mega Deal during the Second Executive Meeting. I'll show you how to present those findings in a way that will grab the attention of the customer executive and maximize the size of your Mega Deal.

CHAPTER SUMMARY

Executives make Mega Deals happen: Working with executives is the single biggest secret to closing a Mega Deal.

Executive Whispering: The art of working with executives (both yours and the customer's) to accelerate progress toward a Mega Deal

Microcommitments: Agreements to take small actions that build momentum toward a much larger decision; closing a Mega Deal is a big decision that customers don't arrive at quickly.

First Executive Meeting: The crucial first meeting with your customer's key executive(s); bring your own executive with you to build rapport and set a friendly tone. This is when you'll ask the customer's key executive to commit to three specific micro-commitments:

1. Agree to conduct an assessment of your product or service.
2. Agree that executives from both sides will meet again at the end of your study to review the results.
3. Agree that you will be given access to their current and past data specific to the use case to be used in the assessment.

CHAPTER 3

THE PROOF OF CONCEPT STUDY

Lars might have responded well to my pitch, but Gunther still hated my guts. Back in his office at Enginex headquarters, he regarded me with a sour expression, like a splatter of bird poop he'd discovered on his windshield after cleaning his car.

"Gunther, to do this assessment, we need access to your data," I said. "Our team has to know your current metrics in order to get Lars an accurate report. We need to know exactly how many hours this process currently requires on your end, what other resources are involved, and how close to the regulatory deadlines you are coming on each submission. Also, I'd like to interview everyone who interacts directly with our product. That shouldn't take more than two or three hours and can be done in a single afternoon."

Gunther's condescending expression didn't change. He pressed his fingers together in a gesture of superiority. His desk, like nearly everything in his office, was a modern combination of matte black and stainless steel. Brushed metal surfaces gleamed at me from every corner of the room. It felt more like the sleek interior of a Mercedes-Benz than a corporate office.

"I'm afraid that's impossible," Gunther said slowly, a sneer touching his lips. "The data you want is for internal use only. We never give this out to our *vendors*. And any interviews you conduct would have to be done under my personal supervision. However, I am quite too busy for that, I'm afraid. Now, is there anything else I can help you with?"

I froze. This was unexpected. I'd assumed that, after getting Lars's blessing, it would be easy to access the data I needed in order to begin the PoC study. Now I felt like a child who'd had my hand smacked away after reaching for the cookie jar.

"But . . . um," I fumbled, panicking. "Lars said you'd give me whatever I needed to conduct this assessment. This information is critical to complete a review and analyze the impact a designated team will have on your business."

"Yes, I'm sure it is," he retorted. "And you'll have to make do without it. Good day."

Gunther turned away and busied himself with his laptop. This was my cue to go. Except I didn't. I was starting to get *mad*. I didn't spend all that time gaining approval for the PoC from Lars, the EVP of Gunther's division, only to find myself blocked a few days later.

While Gunther tapped away on his laptop, I pulled out my phone and sent a quick email to my EVP Bill McClellan:

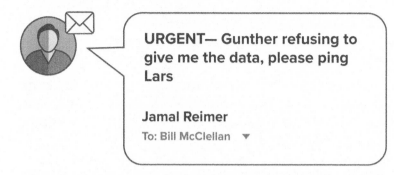

URGENT— Gunther refusing to give me the data, please ping Lars

Jamal Reimer
To: Bill McClellan ▼

Then I turned to Gunther. I was starting to think Lars might have forgotten to tell Gunther about the PoC. After all, he's busy, and it would have been an easy thing to forget.

"What *did* Lars tell you about our assessment?" I pressed. "Did he contact you about it at all?"

Gunther looked up, shocked to see me still sitting across from him.

"I beg your pardon?" He shrugged. "I can assure you, Jamal, this is the first I have heard about any 'assessment.' Now, please."

That confirmed my suspicions.

"Call him," I said, with as much confidence as I could muster. "He will verify everything I'm telling you."

Gunther's eyes bulged. For a moment he seemed intimidated. Then he shrugged.

"Fine." He picked up the brushed steel phone from his desk. "I'll just call him right now."

He punched in a few numbers and put the receiver to his ear. The office was so quiet I could hear the phone ring on the other end of the line. Then Lars's admin picked up.

"Lars Reinhoff's office," she said.

"Hello, may I speak with Lars?" Gunther asked.

"I'm sorry," came the reply. "He's out for the week."

"I understand," Gunther said, and hung up. Then he looked over at me. "He's not in today. I'll try him again next week, and if he confirms what you are saying I'll let you know. Now, please, Jamal. I must get back to work. Thank you for stopping by."

There was nothing else to do. I stood up and clumsily grabbed my things. *Dammit*, I cursed myself silently for being so unprepared. I should have followed up prior to this meeting to make sure Lars had made good on his promise to let Gunther know about the test. The situation could have been avoided with more planning and organization. I grabbed my coat and briefcase and shuffled toward the door, humiliated.

As I walked out, I heard Gunther taking another phone call, already moving on to his next item of business. Except he sounded nervous and on edge. Something was different.

"Lars," Gunther said, "what a surprise to hear from you on your travels."

I stopped in my tracks just outside of Gunther's door and glanced down at my phone. There was already a reply from Bill, and it simply said, "Done."

From inside his office, I could hear Gunther babbling apologetically, and I couldn't help but smile ever so slightly.

"Yes, sir, I just had Jamal here in my office now," Gunther was stammering, "and he mentioned an assessment, but I didn't think . . . Yes, he did mention you by name, I just wasn't sure whether . . . All right, yes, I understand, Lars . . . Absolutely. Have a nice trip, sir. Bye."

"Jamal!" Gunther called out. "Are you still there?"

I turned around, walked a few steps back toward Gunther's office, and stuck my head in the door.

"Yes, Gunther?" I asked, expectantly.

"Lars just called," he said through gritted teeth. "He told me to give you anything you need. I'll email our chief data scientist and a few people on her team who you would be able to interview as early as this afternoon. I'm . . . glad we got that straightened out quickly."

I was overwhelmed with gratitude, excitement, and a feeling of *BOOM, that's what you get for trying to mess with ME.* But I kept my gloating inside as I nodded my head calmly.

"Thank you," I said.

Three hours later, I was back in the top-secret halls of the Enginex crash lab, looking for someone named Annalise Eiker.

"Hello!" She smiled as I stepped into her office. "You must be Jamal."

I was probably the only visitor she'd had all week—maybe all year. It isn't often that a non-employee walks into your office when you work in a high-security facility on the third floor at the end of the hallway.

Annalise's office was a mess. Dirty coffee mugs were scattered about along with notes, readouts, charts, tables, files, and books. Shelves held hundreds of three-ring binders. Posters of famous scientists lined the walls.

"Thanks for seeing me so quickly," I said, stepping around a stack of books and papers on the floor to sit in the empty chair across from her desk. "Gunther says you're the big data wizard around here."

Annalise shrugged. She was surprisingly young and hip to be the lead data scientist for such a large company. She looked to be in her mid to late thirties with short bleached hair, hipster tortoise-shell glasses, a T-shirt, and a brown leather jacket. Her face was soft and kind, and she had a piercing intelligence to her eyes.

"What can I help you with?" She drummed her fingers on the desk. "You said you need some data?"

I handed her a list of the data I wanted, which she glanced at and nodded.

"Can I ask you a few questions too?" I asked.

"Sure," she replied.

"What frustrates you most about the current way your analyses are handled?" I whipped out a pen and notepad from my breast pocket.

Annalise looked off into the distance and thought.

"Actually," she said, "our internal analyses are more frustrating than the stuff you guys do for us. Your team definitely sends reports in at the last minute, which can cause some stress on our end, but they're always perfectly accurate and well formatted. I've never found a mistake in the three years I've been here. With the stuff our team does in-house, on the other hand, I'm constantly finding errors and omissions."

I'd never heard about an internal analysis team. What was she talking about? I was annoyed she'd changed the subject. But then I felt a rush of excitement. *She's experiencing pain*, I realized. *Let's dive deeper.*

"Can you say more?" I asked. "I'm not tracking."

"Well . . ." She thought to herself. "A couple months ago we designed a brake pad insert point using a new aluminum alloy, and the data showed it should hold up against at least twenty-four tons of torque. But when we crash tested it, we found the shearing forces were ripping the component off its housing during collision. Turns out there was an error in the way the odds ratios were calculated during our internal analysis. The new alloy was really only good up to sixteen tons of torque, not twenty-four. We had to scrap the whole project and rebuild the part in carbon fiber, which costs three times more. Then we had to rush production and request new test cars from the manufacturer since we'd messed up the first ones. It was a headache and cost us a fortune."

Mistakes were costing Enginex money. We were on the right trail.

"Any idea what those costs might have looked like?" I asked, trying not to sound too excited about the possibility of discovering another costly problem for Enginex.

Annalise shrugged. "At least two million," she said. "And that's just the most recent example. We deal with these situations every few months. In some ways, that's just the business we're in. There are going to be design flaws, and that's why we test everything so thoroughly. But it's also true that many of these flaws could have been detected earlier with more rigorous analysis."

"What if we could handle those analyses for you?" I asked. "If we bring the same accuracy that we deliver on the work we already do for you on the crash-test side, wouldn't that avoid the kinds of errors you just described?"

"Without question," she fired back. "That would be a game-changer."

I felt like jumping up and pumping my fist in the air. *Yes!* This deal, I realized, could get even bigger than I'd imagined if I played my cards right during the PoC.

"We can do that," I said. "I'm working to build a dedicated team specifically for Enginex, and they could handle all of these statistical models for you, not just crash tests. We're running a sample analysis in the next few weeks, so we could get started right away. All I would need from you is some descriptives on the types of analyses your in-house team runs."

She smiled.

"That would make my day, Jamal," she said. "I'll get all of this together by tomorrow morning."

I beamed. In my head I was trying to determine how much bigger the deal might get if we handled these additional analyses for Enginex as well. If this worked out, it could easily double the size and scope of the deal. It would double the people involved, double the price, and double the impact.

*   *   *

I originally approached Annalise to complete the first task of the PoC: gathering the customer's current-state metrics. But I quickly stumbled onto an opportunity to further expand the deal. It wasn't easy getting a meeting with her, especially with Gunther trying to block me, but in the end, it was more than worth it.

Digging into the Sandbox

After you gain approval from the customer executive to run your test, you'll begin the assessment phase of your Mega Deal pursuit. For our purposes, we will use the term Proof of Concept (PoC) as the assessment type for the rest of this section.

A PoC study is a test you'll run at the customer's site to determine whether your solution has measurable value to their organization. The goal is to find out whether your C-Level Insight applies to the customer like you think it will. At the end of your PoC, you should be able to say unequivocally that your solution works.

The main benefit of the PoC for the Mega Dealer is it quantifies the value of your solution. This allows you to defend your deal size when you face down the customer's procurement team. During the PoC, you'll use the customer's current performance metrics as the benchmark for the exercise prior to implementing your solution and measure them against the improvement your solution brings to compare the difference. As one of the most prominent business thinkers of all time, Peter Drucker, said, "If you can't measure it, you can't improve it." My mentor, Giovanni, has his own version of that phrase: "If you can't measure it, you can't price it." The PoC is your opportunity to measure what's going on so you can improve it and price the solution as a factor of the value it brings the customer.

Another important role of the PoC is helping the customer mitigate risk. Big decisions carry more risk and require more due diligence than small ones. A Mega Deal is a huge commitment for your customer, and it carries significant risk. Before they agree, they need to feel they performed due diligence. The PoC provides customer executives with proof they can trust the solution and confidence to move forward with the relationship. After the test, you'll have incontrovertible evidence that your deal is the best choice for the customer.

In Chapter Two, we saw the importance of getting the assumptions of the PoC agreed upon up front so you and the customer can have clarity on the value your solution provides. The first step of the PoC is to obtain your customer's current performance metrics from them. You need to establish the benchmark before you can blow their current reality out of the water.

If you don't get the assumptions agreed on in advance, your negotiating position will be at risk even before the PoC starts because you will not be able to quantify the benefit your solution brings *in comparison to the customer's current performance*. When you deliver the results of your PoC, you'll say something like, "It costs you $5,000 to do this process today. The PoC showed that with using our tool, the costs drop to just $500. So we're giving you an efficiency improvement by a factor of ten." But what if they say, "Oh no, it only costs us $600 today, not $5,000. Your assumptions are way off. The benefit of your product moves us from \$600 to \$500, which is a \$100 savings, not a 10x improvement."

Unless you have alignment with the customer on their current metrics *in advance of the PoC*, you will be at risk of such attempts by naysayers among your customer's stakeholders to discredit or water down your solution's value.

Gathering this data is a great way to get on-site with your customer stakeholders, establish relationships, have one-on-one conversations, hear perspectives, and obtain microcommitments. Along the way you can often find opportunities to further expand your Mega Deal. For instance, on Enginex I wouldn't have learned about the costly mistakes from the customer's in-house analysis team if I didn't visit Annalise in her office to ask about her problems and frustrations. That one piece of information doubled the size and impact of the deal.

Because you started Executive Whispering early in the sales cycle, you already have executive connections and are performing a mutually agreed project, so the stakeholders you engage with can't limit your ability to move around the organization. It's a completely different situation than the mountain hiker seller who is still trying to get a meeting with someone above the Manager level.

With that executive mandate, you don't have to get in, gather the data, and get out as quickly as possible. Don't completely delegate this task to a Presales or Services team member to do this for you. Use this opportunity to get in front of as many stakeholders as possible, get to know them, learn what they do and what their problems are, and establish real relationships. The more you personally invest during this phase, the more likely you'll be to discover a large and expanding opportunity to serve the customer.

There are two ways to look to expand your Mega Deal: expand the scope of use or the scope of solutions.

EXPAND SCOPE OF USE

Try branching out your search rather than sticking narrowly to a single department or team. Some of the best Mega Deal opportunities are built when you expand the potential uses of your offering and implement your solution across multiple business units or companywide rather than just in one particular instance. When I find a customer stakeholder who is truly excited about my solution, I ask them for internal referrals. These players are perfectly positioned to help you—they love your value proposition, they want it for their part of the business, and they very likely know others in the company who have the same problem. Customer supporters of your solution are typically more than happy to introduce you to other potential users of your solution. You are a trusted solution provider working on an executive-mandated project. You have a ton of credibility and momentum in the account. You have a great brand. Leverage it to expand the potential scope of use of your Mega Deal.

EXPAND SCOPE OF SOLUTIONS

If you have multiple products or services in your solutions portfolio, you can have a second bite of the apple by adding them to the scope of the PoC where applicable. In the data-gathering phase, you and your team will get a more detailed understanding of the depth and breadth of the customer's pains and will see opportunities to position a full solution made up of several components rather than a single product or service.

When it's executed properly, looking to expand the use or number of solutions allows you to grow your deal significantly by proving outsize value. If it wasn't a Mega Deal at the outset, it certainly will be when you get through with your PoC.

Four Categories of Value

There are four high-level categories of value listed below in a loose order of priority that most organizations follow:

FOUR CATEGORIES OF VALUE

1

Make or save money or other resources like time, power, raw materials, space, or bandwidth

2

Improve the quality of the customer's outputs, such as higher durability, greater accuracy, decreased latency, or a product that is sharper, cleaner, bigger, shinier, or otherwise better

3

Offer a better experience for the customer's employees or other stakeholders, including less frustration, fewer clicks, more interactivity, better support, or a more attractive interface

4

Provide a secure environment, process, experience, or outcome for internal or external stakeholders' assets

Any seller can promise their product or service will provide these types of value. The PoC allows a Mega Dealer to *prove* it. To design a proper PoC, you have to dig down to the quantifiable targets beneath these outcomes. Your goal is to produce hard measurements, such as:

CUSTOMER KEY PERFORMANCE METRICS		
Targeted Areas	**Current-state**	**Future-state**
Cost to upgrade database:	**$6,750** (via internal IT resources)	**$23** (via automated technology)
Number of clicks necessary to perform each repetitive task:	19	6
User satisfaction score:	42%	91%
Intrusion detection rate:	86%	99.94%
Cloud infrastructure availability:	97%	99.997%

The table highlights an issue I brought up about what to cover in the First Executive Meeting. If you notice, every example in the table has "current" and "future" numbers. They show the difference in quantifiable business outcomes before and after the use of your solution in a PoC environment. In the First Executive Meeting, I discussed getting agreement with the customer executive to provide access to the current data that measures the inputs to achieving their business outcome. Without that data, we would never be able to produce the table above. At best, we would only be able to show our PoC results with no reference point. The potentially massive impact your solution could have would not be proven, and your Mega Deal opportunity would turn into a small initial deal or no deal at all.

Sometimes after the executive meeting, someone will be tasked with getting you the data but will not have been given any details as to what exact data you need. You'll need to get specific with them by sending them a list of data points you need. You will need to create your own list, but below are the type of questions you will be looking to answer:

- How long does the process currently take?
- How many people does it require?
- What are the direct costs?
- What are the indirect costs?
- Are there bottlenecks that slow down the process?
- Are there steps in the process that are especially prone to error?
- What is the rate of successful completion?
- What is the total number of errors?
- Do you execute this differently than peers or competitors?
- Does the process introduce risks?
- Where are the weaknesses in the process?

The more data you get about your customer's current state, the easier it will be to pinpoint proof that your offering will improve their lives.

Drafting My Team

I looked down at the scribbled list of names clutched in my hand. Most were either checked off or crossed out, but there was one glaring exception right at the top: Vlad. There was nobody with a better reputation for getting complicated paperwork done flawlessly and pushing through impossible approvals than Vlad Malik. I needed him on my team, but I couldn't find him anywhere.

The halls were deserted as I passed by our Approvals department again and peeked into his office. No luck. Vlad was a ghost. He was always off in some random corner of campus, tracking down a certain signature, following up on a delay, or petitioning for an override.

"Jamal." I spun around. Vlad was coming down the hallway toward me. "Good to see you!"

"Vlad." I smiled. "I've been looking for you all day. Are you ever in your office?"

"Not when there's paperwork to be done," he said seriously. "I had to rush our request for a QM-90 abridged supplier vetting protocol on Leslie's new drone automation deal. Normally the board doesn't review those LZ-56 requests until the second Thursday of the month, so I needed eight different signatures to submit an RT-31 and convene an emergency session. That's taken up most of my last two days."

I chuckled to myself. Vlad was exactly who I needed on my team.

"I've got a kickoff meeting tomorrow morning for my new PoC," I said as we stepped into Vlad's office. "Can you be there? I could really use your help with all of the paperwork."

"Tomorrow?" Vlad furrowed his brow in concern. "Jamal, don't you know the approvals process to approve a PoC team member typically takes at least forty-eight hours? Especially this close to the end of the quarter. There's no way I can join your project if the kickoff meeting is tomorrow. I'm sorry."

I froze. That's not a response I'd been expecting.

"But can't you just show up?" I stammered. "I need you, Vlad. I didn't even know about the forty-eight-hour thing. That's how bad I am at this stuff! Please. What can we do? Can we file it right away and you attend unofficially for the first meeting?"

Vlad considered.

"That's strictly against protocol," he said, shaking his head and crossing his arms.

Silence hung in the air for longer than was comfortable. He seemed to be wrestling with the decision.

Then his face lit up.

"I know!" He jumped up from his chair. "I'll override the forty-eight-hour window with an emergency J-16 signed by Leslie, since I was out of the office working on her drone deal during most of the last two days. I know she's still in her office because I was just over there."

He beamed triumphantly as he raced over to the back wall, which was lined floor to ceiling with wooden cubbies holding every form and approval letter our company used.

"Here's an I-36," he muttered, "and there's the J-16."

Then he was back at his desk, reviewing the form while clicking his pen open and closed with his thumb.

"Do you have the customer ID number and contract code for this account renewal?" He looked up expectantly, as though I was supposed to recite them from memory. "We need to get this done right away to catch Leslie before she heads out," he said earnestly.

I located the numbers he needed in my inbox while Vlad filled out the rest of the form. Then he raced out the door, clutching the two sheets of paper.

"See you tomorrow," he called over his shoulder on his way out the door, "at the kickoff meeting!"

And he was gone.

I shook my head and chuckled to myself. Then I unfolded my list and crossed off the final name: Vlad Malik.

With my team complete and Bill McClellan now supporting my deal within the company, things were going to move fast from here on out.

I reviewed everyone who was part of the team for this deal. In addition to Bill, Vlad, and Victor, I also had Giovanni, who had agreed to help me analyze the data from the PoC and develop a story for the Second Executive Meeting. There was nobody better at finding a signal in the data than Giovanni, so I was excited to have his help on this project.

I also had Arun and his right-hand woman, Meghan Graham, on my team too. They represented our Professional Services side of the company. Everything involving our analysts on the Enginex deal was considered services and fell under their domain. They knew everything about our current Enginex engagement, down to each consultant involved.

Representing the software side of the company was my responsibility, and I had a Presales Engineer named Carl Teske to help me. Carl had a deep knowledge of our products, how they worked, and what they could do. He was an expert at understanding the features and benefits of our various options.

Finally, for overall support, there was Giovanni's assistant, Marisol, who organized all team meetings, worked out logistics and travel, and made sure everyone had everything they needed.

I folded up the list and slid it into my pocket. My team was complete, and it was time to head home and get a few hours of sleep so I could come back and prepare for the PoC kickoff meeting.

* * *

During the Enginex deal I learned the importance of having the right team in place. There were many situations during the deal pursuit where members of my team stepped up and filled the gaps in my own knowledge or skills. While I was gradually adding people to my team throughout the sales cycle, the start of the PoC is when I got most serious about curating the members of my Mega Deal team.

The Phases of a PoC

A PoC study has five main phases, and it should take no more than three months from start to finish. The exact timeline depends on the complexity of your solution. You might have a demo version of your product that can be set up and tested in under a week. Or if you're selling an analytics tool, you might be able to conduct the PoC in a single afternoon with nothing more than a spreadsheet from the customer that you run through your software. Other times you might have to set up a customer-specific environment or train their people on how to use your solution before it can be deployed. With Enginex, it took us a week to gather the data we needed, another week to run the algorithms, and three days to analyze the results.

A typical PoC consists of five components:

1. Kickoff
2. Setup
3. Execution
4. Analysis
5. Conclusion

Let's explore these phases in a bit more detail.

1. KICKOFF

A PoC begins with a kickoff meeting, bringing together the combined team, which includes everyone who's going to be involved from your company and the customer's in the same room (remote kickoff sessions can work fine if you're physically separated). The Mega Dealer's job during the PoC is that of the coach, and the kickoff meeting is when you'll first address your team members and assign them positions.

Start your kickoff meeting by recapping the Mega Deal Premise. Walk your team through the Core Imperative, C-Level Insight, and Distinctive Value Proposition to make sure everyone is on the same page about the goal of the PoC, which is: *Does your Distinctive Value Proposition deliver business outcomes that will enable the customer to achieve their Core Imperative?* Explain that the entire sales cycle should run like a well-choreographed play. Your team members will interact with customer stakeholders, and it's important to make sure everyone in the customer's organization receives a clear, simple, and consistent message.

Next, generate a list of all the tasks that will be involved in the PoC and gather input from the team on whether the list is complete. Finally, assign these tasks to people. Ask who wants to be responsible for what and put a name next to each task on the whiteboard.

You've just built your PoC team and conducted the first practice. Good job, coach.

2. SETUP

The setup is often the longest phase of a PoC given the number of tasks to configure the players, systems, and processes for success. This is when you will gather the current data, learn the technical specifications, configure your tech and/or services team, and train the customer on how to use your product or work with your people.

Your first objective during the setup is to establish the PoC environment. The typical host of questions will revolve around access, integrations, and security—all that good stuff that your technical team will handle.

If your solution is services-based, setup is mostly about access and permissions for your team, the beginning and end points of the business process they will execute, and the expected deliverables.

Another key aspect of the setup phase is to poll key customer stakeholders about their experience with the problem statement. By now you will already have the as-is metrics about the business process in question, but what is needed now is firsthand input as to how the process impacts the people involved. Their statements will give the description and detail you need to create a stark contrast regarding how bad it was pre-PoC and how much better life will be for everyone involved once your solution is up and running.

I ask lots of questions of the customer's PoC team. This can be through guided conversation or through a survey. Some examples of questions you can include are:

- What is the most frustrating thing about your current business process?
- What is one thing that would make your process more efficient?
- Where in the current process are errors most likely to emerge?
- What is the one thing you wish you were able to do that you can't do today?
- Of all the steps in the process, which is the most problematic for you?
- What is the impact of the challenges you face with the current process?

Be on the lookout for stakeholders who are especially engaged with the PoC. It will be obvious who is passionate about what you are doing because they will give long and detailed answers to your pre-PoC questions. Anyone who takes the time to walk you through details or who comes up with issues you haven't thought of is someone who is invested in solving the problem. They will have valuable knowledge of on-the-ground realities. If you listen, these people can become supporters who will guide you through the PoC and beyond.

In the movie *The Godfather: Part II*, Michael Corleone famously said, "Keep your friends close, but your enemies closer." This is especially true during the setup for a PoC. Don't get "happy ears" by hanging out exclusively with customer stakeholders who support your solution. Find and engage your detractors as well. If you don't know exactly what it is about your value proposition they object to, you won't know how to address their concerns.

There will be other block-and-tackle tasks that need to happen during the setup phase, which you will not do personally but you will be accountable for making sure are completed by others. Training is an example. Whether you sell technology or services, the customer stakeholders will at least need an orientation if not some level of formal training to know how to play their part in the PoC. This often receives short shrift because the customer stakeholders already have tons of work in their day jobs and if not chased will not prioritize your PoC training sessions. If you allow this to happen, the PoC will be compromised as the customer stakeholders will ultimately get frustrated and blame your product or service. Get in front of the problem by getting their managers to ensure key people show up for training.

Once you've got your team in place and stakeholders trained, it's time to get into a steady cadence of meetings. You want everybody conditioned to regular stand-up meetings. Schedule a weekly thirty-minute call with all of the key people on your team to share updates about the progress of the PoC and the deal.

How often you invite someone to your calls will depend on their seniority. For an executive, it might be once a month. For lower-level players, it's every week. When you've got the team set up and a cadence of weekly calls in place, it's time to begin the PoC itself.

3. EXECUTION

The execution of a PoC can differ widely depending on the specific type of product or solution you are testing out for the customer. Some PoCs are just about moving data, in which case they can basically be conducted from your office. Other PoCs might involve installing software on employee computers at the customer's headquarters. Or you might be providing call center employees with a new headset to try out. One way to conduct a PoC is known as a conference room pilot. To achieve this, set up some machines in a conference room at the customer's headquarters and bring groups of their employees in to try out your solution and answer a few questions about their experience.

The demands and circumstances can vary, but the goal is always to demonstrate massive value.

Here is the thing about the execution phase: the nuts and bolts of chunking away at having your customer stakeholders experience your solution will happen whether you are in the room or not. Execution is typically run by a technical resource or a Project Manager. Yes, you can participate to the level you can, but as a seller I am typically watching the show from the sidelines, taking notes. A better use of my time is to get out and meet with stakeholders who are important to my selling efforts but not directly involved in the PoC activities. I leverage PoC execution sessions as a reason to be on-site (when travel is possible) and to schedule as many meetings as possible to inform stakeholders about the PoC and what problems we are working on and to broaden my network of support for moving forward.

4. ANALYSIS

When you've wrapped up the execution, it's time to crunch the numbers and analyze outcomes. This is when you'll hunt for compelling insights and hone in on impactful ways to present your findings to the customer's executives at your follow-up meeting.

It's important to tell a story with your findings. And this story needs to end with a direct and measurable impact in the achievement of one of the customer's Core Imperatives. For instance, if employee satisfaction is a Core Imperative for your customer, it isn't enough to simply show that your solution saved employees an average of twelve minutes per task, yielding a 7 percent increase in productivity per worker. Productivity is great, but it's not a Core Imperative; employee satisfaction is.

Instead, you have to tie your data to what the executives care about *most*. In this case, you might say, "As you can see, our solution saved your employees an average of twelve minutes per task and increased their productivity by 7 percent. But what was most instructive was the results of the survey we gave all PoC participants. They reported that the new process supported by our software led to reduced feelings of stress, anxiety, and burnout, and as a result, employee satisfaction rose by 34 percent, which is more than twice your goal for the year."

Make the story clear, measurable, and all about achieving their Core Imperative.

5. CONCLUSION

The last phase of the PoC is when you'll go through the results with your team and map out your presentation for the Second Executive Meeting. In Chapter Four, I'll show you what to say during that meeting to move the Mega Deal forward and obtain the next micro-commitment. The Second Executive Meeting is when you'll *finally* deliver your pitch and ask the customer executive to do business together. But you'll see this isn't your typical closing presentation . . .

Running Out of Time

We'd only *just* finished training the dedicated team of analysts for the PoC when a call came through from Enginex: they had a job for us. We scrambled to set up an encrypted network as the data for Enginex's latest crash test poured in. With Lars's support, we routed this job to our bench team in India *and* the new designated team. This would allow us to compare metrics and see which team did a better job. To keep the test blind, we didn't inform either team about the competition.

Part of the reason it took longer than expected to get the team up and running was a cluster of holidays that hit right during our PoC activities. Several of our analysts had been flown in from our European office for the PoC. Just when we'd finally gotten everyone settled, they all took off for a long weekend. Then the following week was Europe Day, a holiday I wasn't aware of, but which our new European analysts definitely observed. By the time we finally had everyone trained and set up it was May 12, and that's the day the new file arrived from Enginex.

Our analysts looked over the assignment and agreed it was more complicated than the typical tests Enginex conducted. This vehicle was the first all-electric car Enginex had tested, so things would be different. We had to start from the basics.

However, that would have to wait because the next two days were two more European holidays, known as Ascension Thursday and Ascension Friday. Apparently, these are recognized throughout the European Union as nonworking days. And since our analysts were employed through our European arm, they got the days off.

By the next week we were way behind. Our team worked around the clock on the analysis. I stressed out like crazy. It was just my luck we'd somehow managed to set up our PoC at the worst possible time: right in the midst of a string of holidays I had no idea even existed. I was worried because our bench teams were mostly in Asia. They wouldn't be limited by the same constraints as our onshore team because European holidays aren't observed there.

A terrifying thought gripped me: what if the bench team actually completed this project *faster* than the designated team? My PoC would be blown and we would have wasted thousands of dollars and weeks of time on a failed experiment.

Thankfully, by the end of the day on Friday the analysis was nearly complete. It was due the following Tuesday by midnight. I figured we could take the weekend off, come back Monday morning, finish up our statistical model, spend a few hours double-checking the output, and still send the report more than twenty-four hours before it was due. That wasn't amazing, but it was better than the last-minute submissions our bench team was known for on these projects.

Monday morning came and I was at the office early, eager to get the project submitted. However, none of our analysts showed up. The day started at 8:00 a.m., but by 8:15 nobody had arrived. The place was dark and empty. I took a few deep breaths, trying to calm myself, but by 8:30 there was still nobody. We had seven analysts and not a *single one* showed up for the most important day of the project? I was livid.

I called up the lead analyst on his cell phone.

"Jamal?" he asked, yawning. "How are you? Why are you calling on a holiday?"

I fell out of my chair.

A *holiday*?

"Oh, excuse me," I mumbled. "I didn't realize. I'm still learning about all of these European holidays. What holiday is it today, can I ask?"

"It's Whit Monday, of course," he said, as if it was the most obvious thing in the world.

"Right, Whit Monday, yep," I said. "Sorry to bother you. See you tomorrow." And I hung up, feeling like an idiot. Then I googled Whit Monday. Turns out it's a real thing. And it's officially recognized as a holiday in the European Union. I erased "Whit Monday" and typed "holiday, Europe, May 26" and pressed Enter. There were no results.

I hoped some disaster had befallen our bench team, wherever in the world they were.

The next day, things went well. Our analysts showed up on time and finished the analysis by 2:00 p.m. We submitted the report ten hours before the deadline. Then the team started working on some other preliminary data Annalise had sent over to see if we could do a better job than her in-house team.

At the end of the week I headed back to Enginex to find out how everything had gone. Walking down the long hallway to Annalise's office, I paused to collect myself. My heart hammered at the back of my ribs. I felt like I was eight years old on the way to the headmaster's office. The PoC, I knew, was not going well.

I couldn't get over how many holidays there are in May in Europe.

Annalise smiled when I walked into her office.

"Hey, Jamal," she said. "I was just looking over the reports your team has been sending this week. Those guys are good. The capabilities of your software really take this to the next level. And I can't believe how quick they are."

"You . . . really?" I asked. "You aren't mad?"

"Are you kidding?" she said. "The model they used to plot this latest stress curve is way beyond what we have the capacity to do here. I can't even imagine the computing power required for this. It's significantly more robust than what our in-house guys did with the same data."

"Oh, right," I said. "Yes, we have the most advanced statistical super-computer on the planet. It cost over $30 million to build."

The most important part of the PoC, however, wasn't the in-house stuff but the crash test. I was scared to ask about that. How had our designated team fared against the bench team? Was there any silver lining in our mediocre performance?

"And . . . um," I worked up the nerve to ask. "What about the recent crash test? How did that go?"

Annalise's expression changed, and she looked at me quizzically.

"You mean you didn't hear?" she asked, frowning.

I decided to feign ignorance.

"Hear what?" I asked, trying to sound as innocent as possible.

"The new team completely saved our butts," she said. "The offshore guys were sending me a bunch of questions over the weekend and expecting an answer on Monday. But we're headquartered in Europe and Monday was a European holiday, so our whole company was off. There was no way to pull the numbers they needed. I finally got back to them by midday Tuesday, but with the time difference it was already nighttime in India. So they weren't able to get it done until Wednesday, which would have caused us to miss our regulatory deadline. Except, the designated team knew about Whit Monday and made sure to send in all their requests by Thursday night. I got them everything they needed Friday morning. They actually got their report turned in a full ten hours *early*, which is unheard of. Like I said, they completely saved us. You came up with this new solution just in time, Jamal."

"Oh," I said, speechless. That wasn't what I'd been expecting to hear at all. I'd been so sure Annalise was going to yell at me for wasting her time with this test, I had no idea how to respond. "That's great . . . And the quality was OK?"

"Flawless." She smiled. "You're a tense guy, Jamal. Has anyone ever told you that?"

I said it had been a long week and excused myself. Then I made a bee-line for my car. My mind was racing like I'd just drunk about five cups of coffee.

Three minutes later, I merged onto the freeway, turned up the music, and screamed at the top of my lungs. All the stress of the week melted away, and I sunk into the seat like a limp noodle.

After all of that worrying and wondering, everything turned out all right. The PoC was a bigger success than I could have possibly imagined. My designated team had not only outperformed the bench team but also actually prevented a $10 million fine.

Now I had twelve hours to figure out how to present the official PoC results to Lars and pitch him on the Mega Deal.

CHAPTER SUMMARY

Proof of Concept: A PoC is an analysis to determine whether your unique insight is applicable to your customer and whether your solution will have measurable value to their organization.

A typical PoC analysis consists of five phases:

1. **Kickoff:** Assemble the PoC combined team and assign tasks.
2. **Setup:** Prep the players and configure the systems and processes for success.
3. **Execution:** Conduct the PoC and track the results.
4. **Analysis:** Hunt for compelling insights and hone in on impactful ways to present your findings.
5. **Conclusion:** Review the results with your team and prepare your presentation.

Value Categories: The buying criteria for virtually every enterprise investment comes down to whether the product or solution offers one or more of four key values:

1. **Make or save money** or other resources like time, power, raw materials, space, or bandwidth.
2. **Improve the quality of the customer's outputs.**
3. **Offer a better experience** for the customer's employees or other stakeholders.
4. **Offer greater safety or security** to users or the organization.

CHAPTER 4

THE SECOND EXECUTIVE MEETING

"This is egregious," said Giovanni, wrinkling his forehead and puckering his lips in disgust. "I cannot work with this."

I clenched my teeth and tried to remain calm. I'd been happy when Giovanni agreed to assist with the analysis of the PoC data, but now he was taking over the entire process and stressing everyone out. I looked around at my colleagues who'd been working around the clock for the past three weeks. Carl and Arun had deep circles under their eyes. Vlad looked lost in the chaos.

"You're right," I spoke up. "It's confusing, complicated, and not telling a clear story. It's crap. But it's the only crap we've got. And in forty-eight hours, I'll be in that room with Lars and Gunther to present the PoC results. We can't fix everything before then. And we all need sleep. Let's prioritize the strongest arguments and go from there."

Giovanni nodded thoughtfully. He leaned back in his chair and closed his eyes. I held my breath, worried the delicate rear legs of the chair might snap under his muscular frame. From the looks on the faces of my teammates, I wasn't the only one.

"Column K," Giovanni mused, not opening his eyes. "Rows 256 to 291. And Column R, Rows 15 through 50. And . . ."

The room fell silent. Nobody spoke. Giovanni didn't move.

"Um," a shaky voice piped up from the back, "is that all?"

"Shhh!" Giovanni raised a finger. "I'm processing."

Of course he was processing. Giovanni was the closest thing I'd ever seen to a human computer. Somehow he'd taken one pass over the vast spreadsheet we'd spent weeks compiling and committed it to memory. And now he was running complex mental analyses while we sat around like idiots.

"G," he whispered after another moment. "Column G, Rows 477 through 513." With that, he rocked his chair forward and stood up. As he did, the room breathed an audible sigh of relief. "Put those three sets of data in a pivot table and send it to me when it's done." And with that, Giovanni was gone.

Sure. You're welcome?

We'd promised Enginex the results of our analysis would be ready in time for my next meeting with Lars. But our team wasn't sure what we were supposed to be analyzing. When we asked Giovanni to explain what we were looking for in the data, he'd just say, "We need to make the data tell a clear and compelling story."

So that's all we knew. But what, exactly, that meant, we weren't sure. And where, exactly, we might find this story, we had no idea. I'm not a data whiz, so I was relying on Giovanni. I'd seen him pull off at least a dozen huge deals like this, and he'd always been able to handle the PoC analysis alone, in his head, so I had confidence he could get it done—even if his style was unorthodox.

Since our company had been working with Enginex for six years, we had massive amounts of data to use in our analyses. We'd kept track of how many tasks Enginex requested each year, how long each task took to complete, how many resources were required, the number of errors within each process, and the quality of the outcome for each task.

To supplement this internal data, I had a few spreadsheets provided by Enginex's chief data scientist, Annalise, as well as from the surveys and interviews I'd been conducting with Enginex's people. I'd identified their Vendor Manager, Leslie, as important on this deal. She was the liaison between Enginex and all of their vendors (including us) and interacted with our people frequently. I'd also discovered Bosko, the Data Aggregation Process Manager, who relied on our product nearly every day but had never communicated with us directly. Finally, there was Gerard, the super-user representative. He was the top user of our software at Enginex.

I interviewed these three individuals extensively along with six other people who used our product. I also asked them to complete a survey about their experiences. All of this data was included on the master spreadsheet along with the hard data we'd been gathering internally.

Giovanni insisted on getting every relevant piece of information into the same spreadsheet so he could study the data in one view. He'd asked us to include Enginex's wish list on the spreadsheet as well. Gunther's team had given us a list of the requirements and terms they wanted in the contract renewal, and we'd tracked them all in the same spreadsheet.

Mainly Enginex was asking for contract terms that would allow for maximum flexibility. They anticipated conducting twenty-four crash tests per year during the upcoming contract cycle. However, they didn't want to be locked in to that number. They wanted to be able to do anywhere between fifteen and fifty tests, depending on how their needs evolved. And they only wanted to pay for what they used. They wanted flexible volume and pricing. This meant the designated team we were suggesting—the solution we *knew* would solve their biggest pains—was the opposite of what they were asking for. When I asked Giovanni whether this was a problem, he shook his head and waved his hand.

"No problem at all," he said. "They don't know what they want. It's our job to tell them. And the story will help us do it. That's why we need the spreadsheet."

Right, the spreadsheet. That beast of a spreadsheet contained well over ten thousand individual cells of data spread across dozens of columns and hundreds of rows. My team and I had done our best to clean it up, but it was, admittedly, a disaster. Many cells were empty or contained question marks. Others had ranges of values like "26k–33k" or words like "low usage" or "very high." It was ugly.

But it was all we had.

Still not exactly sure what I was looking for, I spent most of the next sixteen hours searching for the missing numbers. It seemed everywhere I looked I hit a dead end.

First, I dug into the error rates. Annalise had mentioned the reports she received from her in-house team were full of errors, while the stuff she got from us was flawless. To verify this, we'd sent a sample of both types of reports out for external third-party review. The results were promising and suggested a big difference in errors. However, I was having trouble linking this improvement to a specific ROI. Enginex was wary to share their numbers on fines, recalls, delays, and expenses. I did manage to get some data, but it was cobbled together from different sources and was messy.

Next, I turned my attention to the efficiency data. I knew time was being wasted with our current process of sending every project out to an offshore team. It was clear internally that we'd had to work harder recently to avoid missing deadlines. But we couldn't expect Enginex to take our word for it; we needed numbers. And it wasn't easy to quantify how much time was wasted with the current approach. We settled on going back through every project from the last six years and adding up every delay that would have been avoided with a dedicated team. But this data too was a disaster. Some entries represented the days a project was delayed, while others were in hours of "elapsed time." I needed to convert these all to the same unit so we could compare them to each other.

Finally, I set to work on the flexibility numbers. Because Enginex was asking for significant leeway with regard to how many tests they completed every year, we wanted to analyze whether this flexibility was necessary and how much it would cost to provide.

The thing that weighed down our ability to give them flexibility was building a dedicated team of expensive specialists—this would create a high fixed cost. If Enginex only did a few tests we'd lose money.

So our plan was to compare their projections to the actual tests conducted every year for the past six years and come up with a safe margin of error. But since the tests had all been completed by different teams working in different parts of the world, the data was in different languages. I struggled to compile it into a meaningful format for comparison.

The hours ticked by, and I worked all through the night. Finally, at 11:00 p.m. the following evening, with my eyes bleary and the cells on my screen blurring together, I saved the spreadsheet and sent it to Giovanni. I wasn't worried he wouldn't have enough time to analyze it. Our meeting wasn't until 11:00 a.m. the next morning, and Giovanni was a human computer. I was more afraid we might have gotten some critical numbers wrong or that the stubborn empty cells would turn out to be the most important ones. I still wasn't sure what we were looking for.

An hour later, I got home and collapsed into bed, falling into a fitful sleep. I couldn't shake the feeling that I should have done more. It seemed I'd failed in some way. What would we say during the meeting? We had some arguments, but we didn't have a knock-out punch. I realized I was going to have to think on my feet, which scared me.

Around 1:00 a.m. my phone rang, and I jolted out of bed. Glancing at the caller ID, I saw it was Giovanni.

"Hello," I whispered, tiptoeing out of the bedroom, into the hall, and past the doors of my sleeping children. "How does the updated spreadsheet look?"

"Jamal!" Giovanni was yelling. There was a hum in the background, and I could barely hear his voice over the sound of rushing wind. "Are you looking at the sheet now?"

"Hang on," I whispered, slipping into the living room and firing up my laptop. "I'm pulling it up. Are you . . . on your motorcycle?"

"Just returning home," he screamed over the noise, "from a long hike. I found the most perfect mushrooms for a fresh sauce!"

"Oh," I said, still half asleep, "that sounds . . . good."

There was a moment of silence during which all I could hear was the wind whistling through Giovanni's helmet. Then I got the spreadsheet open.

"OK," I said. "I'm looking at the data."

"Can you tell me," Giovanni yelled, "what does it say in cell C45? Is it $462,977?"

I glanced at the screen.

"Yes," I said. "Exactly."

"That is wrong," he shouted. "It should be $642,977. That is what you get when you add C12 through C24, right?"

"Hang on," I said, amazed, once again, at Giovanni's brainpower. I quickly added the numbers he mentioned and, sure enough, the sum was $642,977, but the value in the spreadsheet had been input manually and was wrong. "Yes. You're correct. That appears to be an error. I'm sorry about that. I thought we caught everything, but we're all so tired I'm sure we missed a few—"

"Jamal," Giovanni interrupted. "Shut up! It's OK. I've got it! Just had to verify my math. You hear that, Jamal? I've got it! I have figured out our story!"

"That's wonderful," I said. But I had no idea what he meant. And honestly, I was too tired to care.

"Get some sleep, Jamal," he roared. "Tomorrow, we will push this deal through!"

Click.

The phone went dead.

My head slumped backward onto the couch cushions, and I immediately fell asleep.

*　　*　　*

In order to nail my pitch during the Second Executive Meeting, I knew I needed to make the PoC data tell a clear story ending with an impact on the customer's Core Imperative. Because I'd identified meeting regulatory deadlines as a top priority for Enginex, I had to find a way to quantify the impact our PoC had on the likelihood of missing a deadline. It was my job to produce proof that our approach worked. Since data analysis isn't my thing, I recruited Giovanni to help out.

The Four Mind Model

The Second Executive Meeting is the most important conversation you'll have during the Mega Deal process. This is when you'll show the customer executive how well your PoC went and demonstrate why it makes sense to move forward with a much larger engagement. The meeting takes less than an hour, and by the time it's over, you'll have conceptually sold the Mega Deal to the key decision maker.

Even though the goal of this conversation is to convince a small number of executives or even a single stakeholder to buy into your narrative, don't think of it as just one conversation. During any high-stakes encounter there are multiple smaller conversations taking place under the surface.

To understand how this works, imagine yourself buying a car off the lot. The salesperson tells you about the impressive features of the latest model. You're trying to communicate that his price is too high without giving away exactly how much you have to spend. Meanwhile, he's wondering if he can upsell you on the undercoating and heated seats while also trying to calculate whether his commission will be enough for the new smartphone he wants.

During an impactful conversation what's *really* being said happens beneath the surface. Think of the devil and angel sitting on a character's right and left shoulder in a cartoon. That type of internal dialogue is more important than external dialogue.

I use an approach called the Four Mind Model to think about the inner conversations all humans have as we wrestle with any big decision. Picture four characters that all represent different parts of the human psyche. I call them the Thinker, the Feeler, the Memory, and the Analyst. This approach is based on my reading in the areas of psychology and human behavior, along with my own experiences. It's not tied to any particular theory or study, and I'm not a neuroscientist or psychiatrist. It's a model I've developed that my students and I find helpful for approaching impactful conversations with executives.

The first internal character in every impactful conversation is the Thinker. **This is the part of our brain that collects data and performs cause-and-effect logic.** It's in charge of determining whether a certain course of action would be positive or negative. The Thinker is not a decision maker, it's a polltaker and an aggregator. It scours the brain for data, collects it, and tries to determine what it might mean. At the car lot, as you speak with the salesperson, your Thinker works hard to make sense of the details about the car you're considering, including features, safety information, and pricing.

The second character is the Feeler. While the Thinker is busy getting the facts, **the Feeler determines what emotions each fact triggers**. Does the information spark fear? Surprise? Boredom? Just as the Thinker compiles a report on the logical consequences of a decision, the Feeler raises the emotional consequences of an impending decision.

At the car lot, you might compare how safe you feel in one car to how cool and attractive you feel in another. You might also imagine how your spouse will make you feel about each purchase when you get home.

The third character inside of your head during an impactful conversation is the Memory. **This character gives an account of what you perceive as normal based on what you have experienced in the past.** For instance, imagine you receive an email from a prince of a faraway kingdom informing you he's in a crisis and needs the help of a trustworthy foreign partner to gain access to his bank account, where $25 million is being held. He promises to set aside 10 percent of this sum as a reward if you will help him transfer the funds to a secure Swiss account. He assures you he will be eternally grateful for your assistance and discretion.

The information in this email sounds fantastic. The pros definitely outweigh the cons. So your Thinker will likely view the terms of the deal as favorable. Your Feeler will certainly approve as well, due to a positive rush of emotion at the prospect of an unexpected windfall.

But most people don't respond to these emails—we send them straight to the junk folder. Why? Because your third conversational character, the Memory, scans your brain for any relevant previous experiences. In this case, you might have a few recollections about "request for help" email scams. Maybe you've seen a sitcom where one of the characters is duped. Or perhaps you had a friend fall for something similar in the past. Maybe it's happened to you before. Even though this offer looks fantastic on the surface, you're not going to go for it.

The perceptions from your Thinker, Feeler, and Memory are all submitted to the fourth character for a decision.

The Analyst is the final internal decision-making character. **Your Analyst looks over the reports compiled by your other three**

characters and weighs the decision based on all the information available. Importantly, everyone's Analyst is set up a little differently. For some of us, the Analyst is sitting right next to the Feeler and pays a lot of attention to the emotions for every big decision. For others, though, their Analyst listens more closely to the Thinker, while the other characters are mostly ignored.

Your job during an impactful conversation is to influence the Analyst in your customer's mind. But you can't speak to the Analyst directly. You can only get your message to the Analyst by passing it through the other three characters. Each of these three is looking for and cares about something different. That means you have to deliver your message in a way that it is received well by the three gatekeepers and arrives at the Analyst with their blessing.

The Thinker wants to hear that your value proposition has a low risk and high potential reward. Give the Thinker facts and logical arguments that support a positive analysis of your decision. On the other hand, the Feeler wants to hear that your value proposition will help the customer avoid pain and gain pleasure. Finally, the Memory wants to know whether past experiences suggest a decision will be good or bad.

When the overall balance of facts, memories, and emotions checks out, the Analyst gives a decision a green light. However, when the cons seem to outweigh the pros, or when it's too close to call, the Analyst gives the decision a thumbs-down.

Most of us have similar logical abilities and emotional responses. But we all have a different way of combining these three influences and arriving at a final decision. The Four Mind Model takes this into account, and also factors in the role of Memory. Understanding how Memory influences decision-making is crucial to help you gain an executive's blessing during an impactful conversation.

Psychologists divide memories into two main forms: short term and long term. Short-term memory keeps track of what you're working on this week, the meal you enjoyed for lunch, or the blind date you went on last Friday. Short-term memory is constantly refreshed with new information and cleared of old stuff. If something isn't important or impactful, it will fade from your short-term memories to make room for new ones. The short-term memory has a very limited capacity, whereas long-term memory can span a lifetime.

To motivate others to think differently, we're interested in understanding their long-term memories. These are deeply embedded in our brains and, in some ways, they define who we are. Long-term memories are the things we never forget, like the address of our childhood home or the time we fell for a scam and felt like an idiot.

Challenging long-term memory can be a battle. We get comfortable with our persistent beliefs, leading to deep-seated biases that prevent us from accepting new ideas. Do any of these phrases sound familiar?

"We've always done it like this."

"Well, that's just the way it is."

"That's against our policies."

"That's just human nature."

When we describe something as immovable or permanent, that's our long-term memory talking. Our understanding of the world is largely based on these long-term memories. They can be helpful when they save us from email scams. But they can be dangerous when they prevent us from being open to changes that could improve our lives.

The brain is flexible, but old habits die hard. The longer someone believes something, the more entrenched that belief becomes. That's why it's important to figure out what perceptions and beliefs an executive is holding in their long-term memory, so you can offer experiences that suggest change is a good thing.

By learning about an executive's backstory as well as their past business successes and failures, you can start to make educated guesses about how their Memory will interpret your messages. You can also look closely at some of their past decisions and ask yourself whether their Analyst listens more to the Thinker, Feeler, or Memory. This allows you to focus on the aspects of your message that you know will have the best chance of leading to an affirmative decision.

Talk with people who know the executive you're trying to influence and ask about how he or she operates. After a few conversations, it becomes obvious whether the person is more analytical or emotional. You can say something like, "I'm going to be presenting to Diana next week, and I'm trying to get a sense for how she likes to consume data. Should I send her things in advance, or does she like to have more of an informal discussion? Does she want to see a lot of cold, hard facts and figures? Or does she prefer the high-level story?" It also helps to ask about other big decisions the executive has made and what the deciding factors were in those cases.

Based on the word on the street about the executive, it will be easy to start making choices about whether you should support a certain point using a story about an employee whose life was changed, or a statistical analysis that included hundreds of people, or a reference to one of the customer's previous projects. It never hurts to use all three approaches simultaneously.

The Biggest Pitch of My Life

A car horn blared from the street. Half-dressed, I spat the toothpaste from my mouth and glanced through my bathroom window. The black limousine was already waiting in front of my house. *Does Giovanni ever sleep?* I wondered to myself, half-running down the hallway. I grabbed my computer bag, shoes, socks, and suit jacket from beside the door, and shot down the front steps toward the car.

Giovanni is the only person I know who takes a limo to every customer meeting and is never chastised by senior management or Accounting. The man drives so much business for the company he's immune from expense limits. I once took an UberLUX to a meeting by accident and paid using the company credit card. Big mistake. I received a stern call the following week asking me to cover the difference in price between an UberLUX and an UberX (it was $23.78).

The driver opened the door with a wry smile as I streamed toward the waiting car, shirt unbuttoned, coat flying behind me, hands full of documents, clutching a half-buttered bagel.

"Good morning, sir," said the driver.

I forced a half smile and nodded, climbing in.

Giovanni was already inside, leaning back with his eyes closed, listening to classical music. I figured he was processing and left him alone. Bill was lounging to the side, typing on his phone. He winked at me as I slid into the car and plopped down beside him.

The car pulled out and Giovanni opened his eyes.

"Jamal!" He grinned. "This is it! Today, we pitch them on the deal. The *Mega* Deal."

I had to admit, Giovanni's confidence was infectious. Our PoC data was a jumble, and I was not satisfied with the deck we prepared. I was putting all my trust in Giovanni to get us through. During the next few hours, I was either going to see this entire deal go up in smoke— along with my job—or else I'd have a front-row seat to a pitch that would go down in the history of our company.

I put our odds at around fifty-fifty.

No matter what happened, it was going to be entertaining.

The rest of the drive passed in silence. Giovanni went back to processing, Bill kept typing (I think he was on Instagram), and despite my stress being through the roof, I fell asleep.

A half hour later we were stepping into Enginex's executive conference room and I was pinching myself to wake up. The long nights were catching up with me, and I was a wreck. Lars, Gunther, data scientist Annalise Eiker, and a few other sharply dressed people awaited us. The walls were glass—some frosted, others transparent. A perfectly round table sat in the center of the room.

Like clockwork, Bill sprang into action. He grinned at Lars like an old friend and shook his hand.

"Hey, Lars, good to see you again." Bill winked. "That McLaren out front—is that yours too? Best-looking F1 I've ever seen."

"Bill," Lars said with a chuckle, "this is Gunther, who runs regulatory compliance here."

"Hey, that's right!" Bill lit up, turning to Gunther. "Lars must have mentioned your name about fifteen times already. I keep saying to myself, sounds like we know who's really running the show around here, if you know what I mean."

Gunther shook Bill's hand, unsure of how to respond. One by one, Bill made the rounds and met every person in the room. Nobody was too insignificant or unimportant for Bill to grab them by the arm, lock eyes, and offer a warm greeting and sincere compliment. By the time we sat down the group was in good spirits.

Once again I was floored by this man's ability to work a room. Bill

McClellan had the type of charisma that could turn skeptics into adoring fans.

"I'm going to be honest, folks," Bill said. "Every one of you knows way more about your business than I could ever hope to—by miles. So I brought a couple of guys with me who I think can better speak your language. Do you mind if we have Jamal here kick us off with a quick overview of why we're here and what we've done so far?"

There were nods all around, and then everyone's eyes turned to me.

"Yes," I said. "Thank you. Good morning. Last time we met, Lars expressed that mitigating risk is a key objective at this time. We identified a high chance of missed regulatory deadlines, which potentially exposes you to significant financial risk over the upcoming contract cycle. So we volunteered to conduct a small test to quantify the risk and determine whether a novel approach might alleviate some of it.

"In the process of that test," I continued, "we also noticed an additional pool of risk we weren't privy to previously: a high rate of errors in your in-house analyses that has, in the past, led to expensive mistakes and wasted time. With permission from Annalise, we looked further into this and reviewed a handful of reports to determine the exact dollar amount for your current risk exposure in that domain as well."

"Very good." Lars nodded. "And what have you found?"

"Well," I said, "as you recall, we hypothesized your risk exposure could be reduced by building a local team of analysts, rather than sending your projects out to our overseas bench team. Because this designated team would have downtime between projects, we anticipated they could take over some analyses from your in-house team as well. So we hired a new team for you as a test. Then we conducted a blind experiment whereby the onshore team and the offshore team were given the same project to determine what differences would emerge.

"The results were very interesting," I finished. "Giovanni, can you walk us through the findings?"

I looked over at Giovanni, who was pulling papers out of his briefcase and stacking them on the desk. We'd determined that Gunther and Lars both relied on their Thinker more than their Feeler or Memory. Thus, instead of telling stories, I wanted to spend most of this meeting talking about data. And Giovanni was the man to do it.

"Yes," Giovanni piped up. "The main thing your team has requested in this contract renewal is flexibility. You want to pay as you go and use our tools and services on an as-needed basis to reduce potential spending. However, our data shows such a model is against your best interests. Too much flexibility exposes you to a level of risk that is disproportionate to your potential savings. You see, we can give you unlimited flexibility to request as many or as few tests as you like. Anywhere from fifteen to fifty per year, as you have requested. And that will, indeed, save you a lot of money. In fact, over the life of our next engagement it will save you exactly $642,977 per test."

As he said this, Giovanni picked up the first pair of report copies and slid them across the table to Lars and Gunther. The executives were listening intently. The precision of Giovanni's numbers had grabbed their attention.

"But," Giovanni cautioned, "that is not what you want. Opting for flexibility means staffing a lean team on our side because you may only do a few tests in any given period. A lean team saves money in terms of fixed costs, but it increases the probability of a missed deadline by 77 percent. When you factor in these risks, your tests will become more expensive—by about $1.67 million each based on our assumptions, which have been validated by your team."

With this, Giovanni grabbed two more reports and slid them across the table to Gunther. I had no idea where this was heading, but I had to admit, it was a great performance.

"On the other hand," he continued, "with a *dedicated* team you'd pay $910,000 more per test than you pay now—a significant increase. However, it would reduce the chances of missing a deadline by 78 percent. And that would save you $2.83 million per test. In the end this new arrangement would save you an estimated $61.4 million over the next three years."

And now Giovanni grabbed the third set of reports and passed those across the table to Lars, who was leaning forward, fascinated.

Gunther, unfortunately, was not convinced. He shook his head.

"This is not what we asked for," he snapped. "We want more flexibility, not less. That is what we are here to discuss."

"You *think* you want more flexibility," Giovanni said. "And, I'll be honest, we thought exactly the same thing. That's why these results were so difficult to get together. We were looking in the wrong place. But take a look at these numbers with me."

Giovanni reached down into his briefcase and produced a new stack of papers. As he did, he flashed me a smile. The son of a gun loved this. He was having a blast.

"We have been doing business with you for six years now," Giovanni said. "In the first year, you predicted eighteen tests but demanded flexibility for anywhere between five and forty. We worked hard to give you that flexibility. You know how many tests you ended up running? Exactly eighteen."

He dropped a sheet of paper on the table in front of Gunther.

"Year two," Giovanni continued, "you predicted twenty-four and used twenty-three. Again you demanded flexibility but didn't use it." Another page fell to the table. "Year three, you predicted nineteen and, again, needed exactly nineteen. Year four, twenty-seven predicted; you actually did thirty tests. Year five, twenty-six and twenty-five. Year six, twenty-two and twenty-four." With each year, he peeled another page from his stack and deposited it in front of Gunther.

"But while you saved money by hiring a smaller team of our lower-level consultants, there has been a growing risk of missed deadlines, which has been brought to light by our research. For the past two years, we've met our deadlines by a smaller margin each quarter." Another report slid across the table. "That's the hard data of delivery dates versus deadlines. We also interviewed your team that receives our analysis reports, as well as our own team who produces and delivers them. We learned they often have to break our agreed process to deliver the reports on time. Without adherence to the process, we can't guarantee the quality of the output."

The body language of the audience had become tense. You could hear a pin drop every time Giovanni paused between statements.

"By my calculations," Giovanni went on, "if this trend continues, our combined teams will miss *two* deadlines over the next eighteen months, resulting in $20 million in fines. This would not only wipe out your cost savings from using a lean team, it would also put you in the red an additional $12.7 million. Please, check these numbers yourself. At the end of the day, to address this risk, the data shows you don't need flexibility; you need *speed and precision*. We can deliver both by providing you a dedicated team of our most senior consultants. It will cost more up front, but will save you millions in the long run."

The executives pored over Giovanni's papers, scowling. But he wasn't done yet.

"Let's talk about errors," Giovanni said. "After reviewing twenty-five of your in-house analyses, we learned the error rate is 4.7 errors in every one hundred calculations. When you're dealing with life-and-death collisions, that is absurdly high. Our own reports came in at just .003 errors per one hundred calculations. This improvement will remove an estimated $78,000 of long-term liability risk per analysis, even after factoring in the increased cost. Since you run four to six per week, that wipes another $20.8 million worth of risk off the table every year."

Gunther frowned. "We'll have to check these numbers using our in-house team," he said.

"Annalise." Lars turned to his chief data scientist. "Are these estimates correct?"

"Absolutely," Annalise said, without pausing. "Jamal got all of these numbers directly from me and, honestly, I'd trust their analyses over ours any day."

Giovanni sat back to let the conversation pause. Gunther was deep in thought, looking over the papers in front of him. I knew his inner Analyst was busy scrutinizing Giovanni's data, probing for weaknesses. For an uncomfortable moment, nobody spoke.

Then, ever so subtly, Lars started to nod.

"I have to say, I am impressed with your research," he said. "Tell me about this new plan. What would it look like and how much would it cost?"

Bill took a breath and exhaled thoughtfully. That was his cue.

"Obviously the cost is going to go up." He shrugged. "There's no way around that. This local team will be a lot more expensive. They'll cost on average $250 per hour apiece, whereas the offshore team you're currently using is billed out at $100 per hour. On top of that, since they'll be dedicated, you'll be covering their costs even when there are no active tests. All of that will bring this renewal from $10 million up into the neighborhood of $55 million. At first glance, we know that sounds crazy. But the benefit is that you'll wipe over $100 million in risk off the table every year and see a significant impact in your bottom line and shareholder value. When we crunch the numbers, this is a much better deal for you guys."

Gunther was scribbling notes all over the loose pieces of paper in front of him. Lars was looking off into the distance, thinking to himself.

"Yes, yes, yes," Lars mumbled. "I see, I see. Actually that might . . . If we can get the details right with this . . . That just might work." He sounded contemplative but also extremely excited.

"Let me bring this to my CEO and executive team," he said. "How soon could you write up a discussion document proposing how this new arrangement would work?"

"Very soon," my voice cracked. "By next week." The room was spinning. Adrenaline was pumping through my body. My eyes felt like they were bulging out of my head. Bill had just casually uttered the words "fifty-five million dollars" and Lars hadn't even batted an eye.

I couldn't wait to get back and tell Carl and Vlad everything that had happened today. And I'd have to call Victor and update him too.

But first, I really needed a nap.

*　　*　　*

The pitch that sold Lars Reinhoff on the Enginex Mega Deal took just twenty-five minutes to deliver. But my team and I spent months developing the Mega Deal Premise, gathering data, conducting the PoC, and drawing conclusions. We succeeded because we prepared thoroughly and framed our messaging to appeal to the minds of our audience. Then we delivered the pitch in a conversational way.

Stop Presenting, Start Conversing

The Second Executive Meeting is when you'll share the results of your PoC, and it's important to make this a *conversation*, not a pitch. You're revealing your findings, but you can't let it turn into a one-way presentation. This needs to be a working dialogue.

One of the biggest differences between conversations and presentations is ownership. Who "owns" the ideas being discussed? During a presentation it's clear who gets credit for the ideas: the person presenting. In fact, during most presentations, the presenter is the only person talking. And because everything is voiced by the presenter, all of the ideas obviously belong to them.

Do you get more excited about other people's ideas or your own?

Most of us care way more about our own thoughts, feelings, intuitions, and revelations than about someone else's. If you can help your customer's executives arrive at an idea themselves (even if you guided them there), it's much easier to get them invested in the outcome.

You can make every presentation into a conversation. The key is to get your audience talking and interacting with you and the content, rather than passively absorbing it. Avoid PowerPoint slides wherever possible because they are static props created ahead of time. Use a whiteboard to jot down figures, workflows, and ideas that come up in the meeting. This way it feels like a brainstorming session. Start writing on the whiteboard, and when the customer executive says something, hand them the marker and they will naturally get up and start writing. Now you are creating ideas together. This is what Steve Jobs and Bob Iger did when they went through the pros and cons of Disney buying Pixar.

Also, don't treat your audience like a single unit. I don't like the word "audience." In reality, each of your listeners is unique. Their memories and feelings cause them to have a different internal conversation about your ideas. The best presenters recognize this and tailor their message to each of the key listeners.

Before a meeting, make a list of who will be attending. Ask yourself some questions about each person and use the answers to plan different ways of landing each of your main points so they resonate with everyone.

- Does this executive listen more to their Feeler or Thinker?
- Should I focus more on ROI calculations, or would this person be more influenced by emotional stories about what other customers have gone through or achieved?
- Should I illustrate how my product made past customers look or how it made them feel?
- Would it help if this executive could picture an image of herself in a place of success?
- How can I get my story across efficiently to this person without self-inflicted impediments or resistance to my ideas based on how I present them?
- Which is the path of least resistance through this executive's brain?

Important note: *this is not about how to manipulate people.* It's about presenting your ideas in a compelling way that doesn't create roadblocks in the minds of your audience. Speaking to the wrong part of the brain can kill your chances of success before you get started. You want to tell a story that speaks to the ideal part of the customer's brain—the part that will inspire action.

The best way to find out how everyone in the Second Executive Meeting thinks is to speak with each person individually and do some research on them before the meeting. The rapport and credibility you build through those individual meetings will give you an edge during the big one. During the PoC study is a natural time to connect with everyone who will be attending the meeting and learn what makes them tick. Ask questions and listen for clues about what kinds of internal conversations they are having. Pay attention to their thought process and note whether they use more logical words, emotional words, or remembering words. These are indicators into how they think.

- **Logical words:** I think, the fact is, the data shows, theoretically, the truth is
- **Emotional words:** it feels like, I'm worried, I'm afraid, that scares me, how exciting
- **Remembering words:** last time, previously we tried, I remember, there was a time when

On Enginex, the hours I put in speaking with dozens of stakeholders throughout the PoC paid off big during the Second Executive Meeting when I realized I'd already spent time with every single executive in the room. Whenever Lars needed confirmation of our numbers during the meeting, he looked to Annalise, and she didn't hesitate to back us up with a nod or a few words of affirmation. Even the lawyer and middle managers in the room, whom I was meeting for the first time, regarded me with the same familiarity as the people I had developed relationships with. They adapted to the energy of the group. Every one of those relationships enhanced my brand when it counted most.

The Second Executive Meeting should have an agenda that looks like this:

- Restate the Mega Deal Premise.
- Recap the PoC plan.
- Reveal the results.
- Describe the long-term impact.
- Show the path forward.
- Agree on next steps.

Let's visit all of these topics in detail.

TOPIC 1: THE MEGA DEAL PREMISE

The Second Executive Meeting often takes place months after the first, and there are usually some new people attending. For these reasons, it's always good practice to **start with a brief overview of the Mega Deal Premise**. This means you'll want to re-explain your hypothesis about the relationship between the customer's Core Imperative, the C-Level Insight, and the Distinctive Value Proposition before you discuss the PoC itself.

TOPIC 2: RECAP THE POC PLAN

Next, **remind the executive(s) about the design of the PoC analysis that you both agreed on during the First Executive Meeting**. Walk through the variables you were testing and the outcomes you were hoping to influence. Tell this as a step-by-step story, explaining what you did first, then what happened next, and so forth. Sometimes it helps to draw a diagram here illustrating how the analysis was set up and how it differed from the customer's standard process. Finally, leave off with intrigue, implying that the results were surprising. But don't give away the punch line all at once.

TOPIC 3: REVEAL THE RESULTS

Here's where you'll **dive into the details and share your PoC findings**. Stick to the cold, hard facts here. As Giovanni liked to tell me, "You can argue any point that you can prove with numbers." Walk the executive through the numbers in a four- or five-step sequence. Start with the point of change introduced in the PoC—a different process, a new tool, etc.—and then show how that affected one outcome, which influenced a larger outcome, which had a certain higher effect across the organization. End with a clearly defined impact on the Core Imperative you were trying to target with the analysis and a dollar amount that was saved or generated. For instance, "The new oil blend reduced friction in the ball bearings by 2.1 Ns/cm, leading to smoother action on the soldering arm and a savings of 8.4 kWh of energy per arm, improving energy usage 84 percent and resulting in a savings of $22,760 per day."

TOPIC 4: DESCRIBE THE LONG-TERM IMPACT

It's important not to stop with the results. Look beyond the immediate results of the PoC analysis and extrapolate into the future to show what this change could mean for the company over time. If this solution was applied across the customer's entire business for the next few years, what kind of an impact would that have? How would it make their company more competitive in the marketplace? It's important to **show the executive how your deal would offer a business transformation, rather than just an incremental improvement**. For instance, "If we made these changes across your production facility, we could save you upwards of $25 million per year and reduce your carbon footprint by half, making you a leader in eco-friendly fabrication and giving you a financial and moral edge in an increasingly competitive marketplace."

TOPIC 5: SHOW THE PATH FORWARD

Once the customer sees the transformative effect your solution provides, it's time to pitch your Mega Deal. Except, don't race to overcome objections and press for a signature right away, like many sellers do. A Mega Deal is a longer game. Instead, **explain to the customer exactly what it would look like to work together to achieve the goal**. What would the project phases be? How long would it take to implement? How much effort would be needed from the customer? For instance, "We'd roll out our plan in five steps: set up your environment; configure the application; train users; run a pilot with ten users; and then, after the configurations have been optimized in the pilot, take the application into production across all users, measure initial results, and iterate to create further improvements."

Next, discuss what you've learned from previous implementations. This will show the customer you've taken the journey before and know where the risks are hiding and how to deal with them. This part of the conversation will go miles to establish both that your product or service is right for the customer *and* that you and your team are the right people to make this happen. If you can't refer to previous implementations because you've never done this type of deal before, you'll have to do your first deal for a good price to pave the way for future deals.

TOPIC 6: AGREE ON NEXT STEPS

Finally, get the executive(s) to commit to what's happening next. Before leaving the Second Executive Meeting, secure four more microcommitments:

1. Agreement for ongoing access to the executives
2. The customer's purchasing requirements

3. How to get buy-in from other stakeholders
4. Agree to a tentative timeline to contract signature, implementation, and go-live

Executive Access: With the successful implementation of a C-Level Insight addressing one or more of the customer's Core Imperatives, you've reached trusted advisor status. You've earned the right to make a few suggestions. Use that power now to make sure those lines of communication will stay open throughout the remaining steps in the process.

Before the PoC results meeting, I often suggest to my executive that they should swap contact details with their customer counterpart and make a plan to talk periodically going forward. The reason for this is to open another direct path to a top decision maker. This is critical during the next phase of the Mega Deal, when lower-level players (especially in procurement) may attempt to cut off your access to customer executives.

Buying Requirements: Every company has a buying process with controls in place to ensure they buy efficiently and at minimum risk. And every executive knows how to get around these hurdles when they really want to. Before you leave the Second Executive Meeting, clarify the remaining steps you'll need to follow to get approvals and funding. Agree on a timeline to move through them. When senior management is excited about your solution, they will find creative ways to fast-track the buying process and reduce the effort needed on both sides. If you don't bring it up when you have the executives in the room, you're setting yourself up for the longest possible trip to the finish line.

Key Stakeholder Buy-In: For a Mega Deal, you will undoubtedly trip all the alarms for scrutiny across a long line of customer stakeholders—business leaders, user groups, procurement, legal, security, compliance, etc. By now you will know some of them well, but before you leave the meeting, quickly run through the list of key stakeholders to make sure you know the names of everyone whose blessing you will need to get the deal done.

Timeline: No one can set a deadline like a senior executive. But they don't respond to arbitrary timelines imposed by vendors. If your customer has a sense of urgency due to an internal compelling event, you're in an enviable position. Otherwise, you'll have to create a compelling event yourself.

Compelling events are deadlines based on credible time limitations. The strongest compelling events are customer-driven, like the date they want to launch a new system. Another example would be a contract expiration, which is the compelling event I used on the Enginex deal. An additional compelling event I added was the end of our fiscal year and the fact that the deal would have to be renegotiated from scratch if we pushed it to the next fiscal. To get an executive on a timeline, you need a credible story for your compelling event.

On Being Prescriptive

Being prescriptive means saying *exactly* what must happen and how, especially by giving an instruction.

I raise the point here because being prescriptive is a rare skill among individual contributor sellers and a vital part of influencing senior executives. Leaders respond to people who have strong views and who can back them up with facts, expertise, and experience. They are looking for experts to shed light on confounding problems they haven't or can't figure out on their own. If you can't point the way to the destination and be clear on why yours is the right path to take to get there, who will follow you?

Most sellers are afraid to be prescriptive. Either they feel they do not know their customer's reality well enough to give specific recommendations (lazy rep, hasn't done the homework), or they fear they will offend the customer who might say, "Who the hell are you to tell me what to do?" Or the seller would want to cover all bases by saying, "Our product can do anything around this use case—what do you want it to do?"

They position what their solution *can do* versus exactly how the customer *should* use it, and that is a huge turn-off for senior stakeholders.

Mega Dealers, on the other hand, use their expertise and knowledge of the customer's business to guide them step-by-step as to how to proceed. Also, Mega Dealers explain exactly what the customer should expect to see going forward. What will the first step be? And then what? When will they see results? How long should the process take? Lay it all out.

The sense that you are trying to convey is that although your customer knows their business very well, your organization knows one small corner of their world better than anyone else on the planet. And that deep focus and expertise creates an opportunity for significant business leverage. But there is a particular approach that needs to be taken to unlock that value. You have mastered it and are ready to guide your customer through that process to achieve a unique and desirable result.

Through your efforts in the PoC, you have earned the right to be prescriptive with the customer. Prior to the results of your PoC, it's not a good idea to be too prescriptive with your customers. You don't have meaningful knowledge of their specific reality. They don't trust you yet. However, once you have data, it's time to move into the driver's seat. You've earned the right to make a strong recommendation at this point.

When taking the prescriptive approach you can move away from a sales pitch and into a consultation. You are no longer making your *product* the center of the discussion, but rather the primary topic is the current reality of the customer's business performance and how best to improve it.

Think of how you feel when a doctor writes a prescription for you after diagnosing you with a certain illness or malady. The medication she is recommending might cost hundreds of dollars, but you don't feel like it's a sales pitch. Doctors follow a similar procedure to Mega Dealers. First, they examine you very closely and conduct tests on you. Then they tell you an insight about what is causing your problem and they offer you a way to make it better by employing a therapy or having a procedure.

Prescriptions from doctors are specific. The doctor tells you exactly how many days to take the medication and how many pills you'll need. She doesn't send you off to buy as many pills as you feel like. She makes a specific recommendation and gives you a step-by-step guide to implement her prescription.

Your Mega Deal prescription should be the same way: test, evaluate results, then deliver a prescriptive recommendation of how to produce a superior outcome.

* * *

By the end of the Second Executive Meeting, one of your goals is to reach an agreement with the executive to verbally assent to your deadlines for contract signatures, implementation, and go-live. Make sure to remind the executive of the timeline you established during the First Executive Meeting and the fact that this deal needs to be wrapped up within a specific amount of time for a certain reason. Cite your compelling event at this point, but keep it subtle. For instance, "Glad you're interested in working together. Everyone on my side of the table is excited about this partnership too. On your end, what are the next steps to make sure we are ready to go live with the new business process by the time our current contract ends, which is the end of December?"

Now you're nearing the end of the Mega Deal process, and if you haven't already, you will be getting ready to engage with the customer's procurement team to defend your pricing and terms and prepare final documents to be signed. I've seen too many Mega Deals fall apart or get whacked down in size under price scrutiny. However, this can be avoided with preparation. Before your deal winds up in procurement, there is one more step to complete: you need to gather individual buy-in from every key decision maker on the customer's side. I've got a straightforward approach to identify and gain buy-in from them all. That's the subject of Chapter Five.

CHAPTER SUMMARY

Impactful Conversations: In a conversation, both parties share and own ideas. In a pitch, the ideas are the presenter's alone. Conversations are the best form of communication to influence thinking and motivate action.

The Four Mind Model: How to address the four major parts of the human psyche that create opinions and decisions—the Thinker, the Feeler, the Memory, and the Analyst.

Second Executive Meeting: During this meeting you will reveal the results of the PoC and quantify the impact of your solution. This is the moment to provide the tangible, measurable proof that your solution will have a transformative impact on the customer's business. At least one senior customer executive must attend this meeting.

Agenda: The agenda for the PoC results meeting should include the following topics:

- **Restate the Mega Deal Premise:** Remind the customer of the Core Imperative, C-Level Insight, and Distinctive Value Proposition.
- **Recap the PoC Plan:** Review the process and methodology of the PoC.
- **Reveal the PoC Results:** Detail the PoC results.
- **Describe the Long-Term Impact:** Extrapolate the impact of the new process, solution, or service across as large a scope as possible to maximize customer benefit.
- **Describe the Path Forward:** Walk the audience through your recommended path to the future state scenario.

- **Agree on Next Steps:** Recommend and agree on next steps to execute the deal:

    1. Agreement for ongoing access to the executives
    2. The customer's requirements to buy
    3. How to get buy-in from other stakeholders
    4. Timeline

CHAPTER 5

BUILDING STAKEHOLDER BUY-IN

Enginex's CFO Andre Veldspar was the next level of unreachable. When I asked Lars's assistant for advice on how to get a meeting with Andre, she just laughed. When I asked Annalise the same thing, she told me I had a better chance of getting a lunch date with the pope. I didn't bother to ask Gunther.

Andre was the Chief Financial Officer for a company with over a billion dollars in annual revenue, so it made sense he didn't just leave his office door open for sales reps to pop in and have a chat. But it wasn't just me who couldn't get ahold of the guy; it was everybody. None of my contacts at Enginex could get me close to Andre. Nor could any executives from the companies for which he served on the board of directors. I hadn't reached a dead end; I'd never made any progress at all.

Andre was at the top of my list of important decision makers for my deal. Before anything over $20 million could be finalized at Enginex, it had to be approved by Andre. I'd learned this usually meant his assistant would bring the papers to his desk along with a brief from procurement saying it was the best possible price. That typically satisfied Andre's desire for financial oversight, and he would sign it.

But I didn't want to be dependent on the recommendation of procurement. I wanted to establish a positive perception of our solution for Enginex *independent* of procurement by getting buy-in from the key decision makers ahead of time so the negotiation team couldn't squeeze me on pricing. And most of the decision makers were on my side. Andre was the final piece of the puzzle. Well, Andre and Gunther.

Andre was never around the office because he was constantly traveling the world for finance conferences, board meetings, and networking events. In addition to overseeing the company's budget, he also oversaw their largest contracts with auto manufacturers, and he spent much of his time visiting factories to meet with CEOs and executives.

I thought about giving up on my hopes of reaching Andre. After all, I already had approval from Lars and half a dozen other key people within Enginex. Was there really much benefit to obtaining a verbal yes from this last individual? But even as I tried to talk myself out of it, I knew the answer was yes. Andre was influential within Enginex and had final say on the budget. If he liked my deal, the chances of getting it approved at the number I wanted were much higher.

There wasn't a good pretext to ask Lars to introduce me to Andre. He'd already told me he would run the deal by the CEO and start the procurement process. The ball was in his hands, and it would be rude to imply he needed my help getting it to the end zone. Plus, the reason I wanted Andre's blessing wasn't that I didn't think the deal would go through without it, but rather that I wanted the extra leverage of being aligned with Andre on my solution's value during pricing negotiations.

I reached out to everyone I knew who'd done business with Enginex, but I couldn't find anyone with a direct line to Andre. Apparently, he was only involved in the very largest deals, and none of my contacts had engaged with Enginex at that level. Next, I looked for anyone with a connection to a C-level executive at a major automaker. I figured it was possible to get connected with someone high up in one of these companies who had a relationship with Andre and could make a casual introduction ("Hey, I heard Jamal is working on a big deal at Enginex, small world!").

These efforts all fizzled out too.

That's when I turned to social media. Andre had a private Facebook profile, unused Twitter account, and a LinkedIn page where the latest post was over three months old. He wasn't exactly active on his social channels. LinkedIn seemed like the best place to reach him online, so I combed through everything Andre had ever posted and noted his attitudes and thought patterns. During the past year he'd posted and commented on six articles, and three were related to conducting accurate risk assessments at scale and reducing risk exposure. I recalled Lars mentioning that reducing risk exposure was one of Enginex's main objectives and realized this topic was a perfect tie-in to our current deal.

Over the next couple weeks I read everything I could find about risk exposure, and I began to pepper my own LinkedIn feed with posts about corporate risk assessment, management of risk, and reducing risk across a business portfolio. But I still needed to make a connection to Andre.

That's when I finally caught a break. Andre posted a link to a one-minute video clip from a talk he'd given recently. The topic was compliance and risk assessment for major corporations, and he specifically mentioned that the easiest way for a large company to increase profitability is often to reduce risk exposure rather than increasing revenue.

This was a perfect opportunity. It was current and topical. People are always excited to learn what others think after they post something, and I knew Andre was only receiving four or five comments per video, so I was confident that any comments during the next twelve hours would get his attention.

But instead of commenting on Andre's video myself, I sent a message to Giovanni, asking if he could get our CEO to comment for me.

IMPORTANT Can you pass this along to Sian?

Jamal Reimer

To: Giovanni Lamere ▼

Giovanni, quick favor. I found a way to get to Enginex's CFO! Can you ask Sian to post the following comment and make sure to tag me? Tell him it's for a $50m deal; I think it will work better if it comes from you than me.

Thanks, Jamal

Most relevant ▼

Sian Blackstone • 1st
CEO, Zerlegen

Couldn't agree more, @Andre, great analysis. I had a similar realization while leading our GDPR compliance initiative. What's your take on the direction of AI in protecting personal data? @JamalReimer

Two hours later I got a ping from LinkedIn informing me that Sian Blackstone, the CEO of our company, had made a comment on Andre's post. Now it was time to wait. I was confident Andre would notice that the chief executive of a Fortune 500 company commented on his LinkedIn post. Still, the next few hours were excruciating. I checked my phone every sixty seconds, hoping for a response, but nothing came through. I went to the gym to burn off stress. Still, no reply materialized.

Then, as I was walking through the parking lot, my phone chirped. I yanked it out of my pocket, dropping my gym bag on the ground, as my phone chirped a second time. Glancing at the screen, I saw two notifications from LinkedIn. First, Andre replied to Sian:

Most relevant ▼

Andre Veldspar • 2nd
CFO, Enginex

That's a longer conversation.

Next, Sian sent me a direct message:

Most relevant ▼

Sian Blackstone • 1st
CEO, Zerlegen

Andre just sent me a connection request...

I actually let out a whoop, right there in the parking lot. Then someone honked at me and I realized I was blocking traffic. I ran over to my car to finish celebrating in private.

*　　*　　*

Even though Lars told me he liked my proposal and wanted to move forward, the deal wasn't closable just yet. I still had to get it approved by numerous people within Enginex. By asking around about the company's procurement process, I learned the CFO, Andre, was one of the most important executives whose blessing I would need. I call the process of identifying and connecting with people like Andre building stakeholder buy-in, and it's a critical phase of the Mega Deal process.

Build Stakeholder Buy-In

During the PoC you might interact with dozens of people within the customer's organization, and many will be curious about your findings. After you've shared your results in the Second Executive Meeting, it's a perfect time to go back to all of those people and tell them what you found. Each person you reconnect with has the potential to become an ally who can speak up at the right time to help push your deal through procurement. Gathering buy-in before the deal ends up in procurement will gain you momentum and make closing inevitable.

A stakeholder is anyone at the customer's company who would be impacted by your deal. Building buy-in among stakeholders is a natural component of any sales cycle, but with a Mega Deal the process can be complex and the number of stakeholders involved can be large. There might be hundreds or thousands of people at your customer's company who will be impacted by your deal, making it impossible to interact with all of them. When your deal reaches procurement, they will often restrict your communication with everyone else at the company until the deal has been finalized to take away your visibility into their decision-making process. Thus, the buy-in phase of a Mega Deal can end abruptly when the procurement phase begins.

Building buy-in for a Mega Deal is very much like running a political election campaign. The goal is to win more votes than any other candidate. The field of play can be huge. I have worked on deals where the decision maker consulted tens of executives and surveyed hundreds of staff members for their opinions, so they all had various levels of influence over whether or not I received the contract.

There always seems to be a handful of undiscovered customer stakeholders whose approval you'll end up needing unexpectedly. Either you don't know these people exist, or you haven't realized how much influence they have. Identify those people, engage with them, and either gain their support or at least mitigate their resistance.

I've dropped the ball by underestimating or overlooking a key customer stakeholder, and I've lost deals because of it. So now I invest significant effort into looking for hidden centers of influence within the customer's company before I try to close any deal. Here are the six best things you can do to flush out the most elusive stakeholders:

1. Be on-site when conditions permit.
2. Learn their language.
3. Meet one-on-one.
4. Organize group meetings.
5. Put on a roadshow.
6. Create a Preferred Customer Program.

Be On-Site: In order to connect with as many stakeholders as possible, you need to be at the customer's offices often. Given our experience with the COVID-19 pandemic, this may not always be possible, but when it is, take advantage of the opportunity to be present in person. Being on-site makes you visible, keeps your message top of mind, and creates opportunities for hallway conversations, whiteboard sessions, and chats over coffee. With my biggest potential customers my goal is always to get a security pass. With ever-increasing levels of physical security, this is not easy, but it is possible. I was once granted a security badge at my customer's offices simply because I was there so often my main contact got tired of coming to the lobby to pick me up. It completely changed my personal brand with stakeholders at the headquarters. I was no longer "just a sales guy." I had access to the conference rooms, the company-sponsored restaurants, and other common areas. Everyone who saw me sliding my card through the turnstile knew I was a trusted member of the team.

Learn Their Language: Another way to win over stakeholders at your customer's company is to learn their language. That means understanding their internal jargon as well as their values (which you can usually find on their website). When you speak the customer's language, they'll assume you know what's going on because you sound like one of them. The way to learn the language is to meet with as many people as possible and watch for common words and phrases that everyone seems to use without thinking. When discussing specific projects, I always ask for their internal names. Most large initiatives have names, like Project Windward or the Beachhead Initiative, or an acronym like PACE. Once you pick up on these terms and start using them in conversations with stakeholders, you'll blend in at the customer's company. You will become part of the "us" instead of the "them."

Meet One-on-One: Meeting with individual customer stakeholders is my favorite way to engage. Freed from the presence of superiors or subordinates, it is much easier to establish a peer business relationship with a stakeholder. Corporate culture takes a back seat to human interaction, and you can be real, speak in everyday language, relax, and talk about important topics clearly and simply. One-on-one interactions are the bedrock of relationships and are the most powerful way to understand other people's views, concerns, and goals.

Organize Group Meetings: When there are many stakeholders of a similar type (e.g., users, project managers, IT people), group meetings can go far to win over large numbers of stakeholders in one go. Some companies have hundreds or thousands of a certain type of stakeholder, and it isn't practical or feasible to talk with them all one-on-one. In these instances, arrange to present to a large group.

Put on a Roadshow: Your customer may be located in a different geographic area from you, in which case a roadshow is an excellent way to get your message out while still getting the benefits of face-to-face interactions. If you can set up a series of meetings with various current customers and potential customers in the same region, you can often tempt an individual executive or a small group of executives into coming with you on a roadshow. It's easier to get access to senior executives from the customer side when you have some of your own executives attending the meetings with you. A roadshow is a good use of executive time and can create leaps in awareness, buy-in, and senior relationship building.

Create a Preferred Customer Program (PCP): A PCP is a program sponsored by your company for a select subset of strategic accounts that gives them greater access to your best people and resources and gets them involved in your top-priority projects. It could be a premium user group or an industry-specific coalition or a small number of customers who engage in requirements gathering for the next version of your offering. Getting customers involved in PCPs will give them more reasons to be loyal and increase their operational and financial commitment with you. PCPs also offer a special venue for relationship-building. People love to share their opinions. And nothing makes us feel better than having others ask for and respond to our thoughts. When we feel heard and acknowledged by someone the relationship becomes stronger. This is true at the personal level as well as organizationally. Customers know they are one of hundreds or thousands of companies who make up your customer base, but they still want to feel special.

Every customer feels they are different from all other customers (even industry peers). Lean into this perception by working with your strategy and development teams to create PCPs. These allow your biggest, most strategic customers to give input on the product road map and help decide which new features should be added to the product next. PCPs are for special customers, and your Mega Deal relationships definitely deserve that kind of treatment.

Here's how PCPs work. First, the Product Strategy and Sales departments will agree on a short list of strategic customers who meet two criteria:

- They are among your company's biggest revenue sources.
- They best represent the functional needs of their industries.

The customers chosen will be invited to join a small group of peers. Keep it to just three to five customers, because too many players makes the process unmanageable. Representatives from each customer should meet periodically (usually virtually, sometimes in person) with your PCP team to discuss their strategic direction and weigh in on how your solution can best evolve to support their goals. In the case of technology solutions, the customers will also describe any deficiencies they have experienced in the current version and specific recommendations for future versions of the product. Often, customers will get privileged access to early builds of upcoming product versions to test them before a wider release.

I have that kind of relationship with a few key accounts. These buyers have earned the sway to affect the future of our products because they have consistently made large orders. I am able to leverage the customers' input to improve our product offerings, and by doing so I get a chance to show them how much they matter to us. The process makes us feel more tightly bonded every product cycle. A PCP is one of the best ways to demonstrate that you're listening to your customers.

Plus, the simple act of taking action on customer input is extremely impressive because many companies fail to do it. If your customer's enhancement requests materialize in the next iteration of your product, they will love it. Why would they leave a provider who makes the product better for them? Wouldn't it make sense to expand their engagement with that kind of vendor? Companies enjoy doing business with people who listen and make them feel important. It bears adding that the enhancements made should be broadly applicable to your market and not something that just helps one big customer.

While PCPs are for current customers, educating Mega Deal prospects on your PCP program can further differentiate you from competitors. You can invite prospects to some PCP meetings to give them a first-hand look at how they operate and to meet the other customers in the program. When you have a quality PCP in place, your customers will be raving fans and will be the best confirmation to your prospect that your solution and the people behind it are a great choice in a competitive field of suppliers. To start a PCP, simply invite your best customers to a meeting and ask for their feedback about the product. Then take their suggestions seriously and implement them. During the next product cycle, reach back out and set up another meeting. After the second meeting you can formalize the PCP.

Too Busy for Disneyland

"Sorry, Jamal, there's no way I can do that," said Mick, shaking his head. "Are you crazy? I'm slammed and my calendar is booked. I can't take off next week to go help you with your deal."

I squinted my eyes. Harsh afternoon sunlight was glaring through the window, casting dark shadows across Mick's tidy office. He shrugged his shoulders, as if to say his hands were tied. His face was dark and I couldn't get a read on him. Mick was a burly ex-weightlifter, and he bulged through his button-down shirt. But he was also one of our leading software developers, and he designed and built the analytics applications used by Enginex. I needed his help.

"To be honest," he continued, leaning toward me over the desk, "I'd love to go. I've always wanted to take a trip to Disneyland. But my VP wouldn't allow it. Rhonda never goes for that kind of thing."

But it's a massive deal, I wanted to scream. Instead, I nodded. This was a dead end. If I wanted Mick to come, I had to get Rhonda's permission, which would be hard. She had a reputation around the office for saying no.

When we talk about Disneyland at our company, we aren't referring to the amusement park famous for Space Mountain and Mickey Mouse. Rather, we're speaking of an engineered experience we've jokingly dubbed "Executive Disneyland." When a deal is big enough and a customer executive agrees to visit our headquarters, we pull out all the stops.

These trips take place at our global corporate office in the foothills north of Los Angeles, a sprawling campus brimming with manicured gardens and polished-glass buildings. We bring customer executives there for three days of business sessions, gourmet meals, tours, demonstrations, and entertainment. They meet with top executives in our company, and we make them feel special and important.

When our company approves a trip to Executive Disneyland, we also allow the rep on the account to bring select employees to act as chaperones and presenters. These invitations are rare; the average rep might only get to Executive Disneyland once or twice during a career. Because of this, the invites have become a kind of social currency.

I thanked Mick and left his office. An hour later, I was sitting across from Rhonda.

"Absolutely not," she said, before I'd finished speaking. "You know Mick is our best developer. I can't let him go traipsing off to drink margaritas and help you close your deal, Jamal. I'd have to hand his tasks to other employees, and my whole team is already maxed out trying to get our next release out the door. That's not fair. I'm sorry, but you'll have to find someone else."

She was right. It was a big disturbance to pull someone out of the office for most of a week in the middle of their development cycle. But Mick was critical for the stunt I had planned. I had to help her see that.

"Listen," I said, "the reason I got this approved is because this account is important. The executive who is coming for the site visit, Gunther Svedel, is the one person who doesn't like our deal at Enginex, and this is our last chance to win him over in time to get the deal done this year. I've got everything else lined up except for Mick, and I need him because he wrote the AI algorithm that will bring huge value to Enginex. Please, we leave in a few days."

Rhonda scowled at me. Her eyebrows cut across her eyes in a look of contempt. She folded her arms.

"No," she said. "You can't take Mick."

I left, devastated.

Frantic, I spent the next day trying to get in touch with Rhonda's boss, the Senior Vice President of Software Development, Rajat Renne. But Rajat was out of the office and nobody could give me an estimated return date. I sent an email but received an auto-response informing me Rajat was away from his desk. Everything I tried hit a dead end. Vlad couldn't find any paperwork to file that would override Rhonda's decision.

Finally, in exasperation, I pulled up the company org chart to see who was above Rajat in the pecking order. And I saw a familiar name: Executive Vice President Bill McClellan.

I sent a quick email to Bill asking if he could do anything to help with Rhonda, but I wasn't optimistic. He was two steps above Rhonda and wouldn't want to get involved. Also, I hadn't spoken with him for weeks, and he didn't fully understand how much was riding on this trip to Disneyland. A day later I still hadn't heard from Bill.

Finally, less than twenty-four hours before we had to leave for California, I turned my attention to preparing for the trip. We needed a detailed agenda outlining what the customer executives would be doing every hour of each day. I had to prepare everyone who was going to speak. Without Mick I had a hole in the lineup, and I spent hours on calls with our people in California, hammering out last-minute details.

The next morning on the way to pick up Enginex's people for our flight I got an email from Bill.

Handled

Bill McClellan

To: Jamal Reimer ▼

He'll meet you at the airport

I was shocked. Did this mean Mick was cleared to come on the visit with me? My heart started thumping. Maybe this trip had hope of working out after all.

We stopped at Enginex and everyone who was coming with us piled into the shuttle. Gunther led the way, followed by Annalise Eiker and two analysts. For my own part, I was bringing Giovanni, Arun, Carl, Vlad, and now, I think, Mick. As the driver pulled away from the curb, Giovanni joked that the shuttle ride was like being back in the bus on the way to school, but with a *few* more perks. We were riding in an executive shuttle bus fitted with luxury amenities such as first-class seats, four-person tables, a minibar, onboard Wi-Fi, and high-resolution screens. The banter was natural, and it seemed we were off to a great start. I hoped the good vibes would last.

At the airport we breezed through security and, sure enough, Mick was waiting at our gate.

"I don't know how you did it, Jamal," Mick said as we shook hands. "One minute I'm sitting there, writing code. Then I get a call out of nowhere from Rhonda who tells me to pack up and get to the airport this morning for your Disneyland trip."

I made a mental note to send Rhonda a premium spa treatment gift card to make up for the headache I'd caused her, then I introduced Mick to the Enginex folks and we all boarded the plane.

The rest of the trip went off just as we'd planned. First, we had a tour of the main supercomputer from the actual engineer who designed it, Harlan Chan. He gave us a behind-the-scenes look at how the behemoth processors function, and he blew our minds with how many calculations it can run in a millisecond. Then we sat down for a talk with Arun, who discussed the new dedicated team and explained why it was so much more efficient than the offshore model. He also had bios ready for each of the dedicated team members and handed them out in formal dossiers, one for each Enginex participant. Next, we met with Sian Blackstone, the CEO of our company. He asked Gunther sharp questions about Enginex's business and plans for the future and shared our strategic direction and road map.

Between every meeting there were buffet breakfasts, catered lunches, and steak dinners. In the evenings there were happy hours, dancing, and an exhibition baseball game. The entire three days felt like being in college again.

But I couldn't tell how Gunther was reacting. The guy was impossible to read. His face was always stern and disapproving, no matter what he was doing. I didn't see him smile once or express enthusiasm for anything we were doing. He seemed perpetually deep in thought.

Finally, it was time for the grand finale: Mick's presentation. We gathered in the main theater on campus, a state-of-the-art four-hundred-seat auditorium with a stunning floor-to-ceiling LED screen behind the podium. Beyond that were glass walls and a glass ceiling, through which I could see the sun setting over downtown Los Angeles. A thin haze hung over the city.

Mick started with an awe-inspiring look at the revolutionary new artificial intelligence tools he'd developed and patented, based on discounted reinforcement learning. He told the story of how he originally discovered his ideas and why the process requires a supercomputer in order to be effective. Next, he walked us through a look at our product road map and the changes he expected to make over the next three years.

Just as I'd hoped, Mick's presentation was sensational. He was a charismatic MIT grad who double majored in physics and computer science. He also earned a master's at Carnegie Mellon in artificial intelligence. Before joining our company, he'd spent five years on a top-secret project "funded by the government." That's all we could get him to tell us about it. Mick was a savant.

The reason I knew Mick's participation was so critical for this whole experience was that the AI used in our analysis is one of the main things that makes our value proposition distinctive. It's what made our analysis work for Enginex so accurate. And nobody else has this technology. Mick developed it right here, for us. I wanted Gunther to be very aware of the things that set us apart. Another big distinction was the supercomputer where we ran the analytic models, which we had toured with Gunther earlier in the day.

After Mick's presentation ended, the people from Enginex thanked Mick but had almost no other comments. We loaded everyone into a shuttle and headed for the airport. The group was quiet during the drive. Nobody mentioned what they thought about everything they'd seen during the trip, and I didn't want to ask.

At the airport, as we parted ways to head to our different flights, Gunther shook my hand.

"I think we can all honestly say," he said, loud enough for everyone to hear, "this was the best business trip we've ever had. We loved every minute, from touring the supercomputer to meeting the CEO, and Mick's presentation was so thought-provoking . . . Well, we are still digesting the possibilities of the technology. Jamal, I can't thank you enough for putting this together." And as he let go of my hand, Gunther actually cracked a muted smile.

*   *   *

I realized during the Enginex deal that gaining buy-in from all key stakeholders meant I would have to win over even the skeptics and blockers. In fact, the people who were against my deal were arguably the most important ones to convince. Sooner or later that meant I would have to get Gunther on my side. Because he was the final hold-out on a huge deal, I pulled out all the stops. Everyone on my team pitched in to help bring Gunther on board—and our efforts paid off.

Buy-In Is a Team Effort

Customers might *buy* your product because it solves a problem, but often they *keep* your product because they like having a team of experts to help them realize the product's full potential. The members of a seasoned Mega Deal team not only have detailed knowledge of the product but also deeply understand the customer and industry and they have relationships with people at the customer's company. It'll be hard for your customer to consider competition if your people are deeply engaged with theirs. It is always worth the effort to involve your team in gathering buy-in.

The buy-in process for a Mega Deal is more complex than for a typical deal. In the world of Run-Rate Selling, most enterprise reps are paired with a Presales partner and operate as a two-person team, with one focusing on knowledge of the product and the other focusing on the sales process. That setup works great with deals up to a few hundred thousand dollars, but it's inadequate for Mega Deals. The more money is on the line, the deeper a potential customer is going to want to look under the hood. As deals get bigger, more people are required to address the concerns of all customer stakeholders and to scrutinize your solution, its features and functions, the architecture, your documentation, data governance, and various additional factors. To close a Mega Deal, you must communicate a realistic plan, delegate responsibilities to others, manage multiple teams, and meet tight timelines. These are the skills needed to make it through the buy-in phase.

When you're looking to achieve stakeholder buy-in, focus your energy on the key influencers and decision makers. Document the stakeholder landscape in an org chart tool. Once you have all the players in one view, assign a five-star rating system to signify their level of buy-in: four or five stars for supporters, three stars for neutrals or undecideds, or one or two stars for blockers.

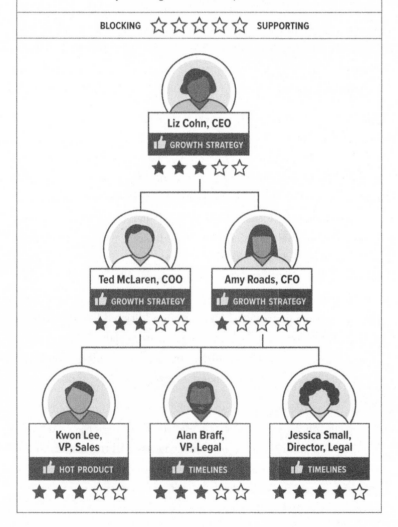

CHART OF STAKEHOLDER BUY-IN

By creating a subjective org-style chart like the one below, you can track the executives that require buy-in, the pain points or the value they see in your solution, and how you think they rate your Mega Deal concept overall.

BLOCKING ☆☆☆☆☆ SUPPORTING

Liz Cohn, CEO
👍 GROWTH STRATEGY
★★★☆☆

Ted McLaren, COO
👍 GROWTH STRATEGY
★★★☆☆

Amy Roads, CFO
👍 GROWTH STRATEGY
★☆☆☆☆

Kwon Lee, VP, Sales
👍 HOT PRODUCT
★★★☆☆

Alan Braff, VP, Legal
👍 TIMELINES
★★★☆☆

Jessica Small, Director, Legal
👍 TIMELINES
★★★★☆

An org chart is a great tool to help you visualize the landscape of your deal on a single page. You can tally up your votes and see if you are on track for a win. If not, dig deeper and ask how you're going to get more buy-in from stakeholders with a low star ranking. I use org charts in internal meetings all the time to discuss deal progress with my team and my management. It's a great tool for getting your executives on board to help sway key players. If Amy the CFO is a blocker, you might ask your head of finance to speak with her. Your CFO will speak Amy's language and will have peer status with her.

You can also dig for motivation to better influence the blockers on your map. Why might Amy be resistant to your deal? Maybe she doesn't like it because the contract will reduce the number of finance people in her department. With enhanced efficiency, her kingdom is going to shrink. She could lose three people because your solution makes them obsolete. Naturally she reacts with, "No way. That's my team. I don't want to lose them. I oppose this deal." Uncover these motivations, then send a finance person who speaks Amy's language to talk with her. You might be able to change her mind and help her see the benefits in your value proposition that make things better for her.

Your CFO could credibly say, "It's true, your team is going to get smaller, but you're going to increase your scope in a couple other areas. You could focus on more strategic initiatives that may have an even greater impact than your team's current responsibilities." Suddenly Amy realizes the potential upside of the initiative because it was shared with her by a peer in the same field, not just a "sales rep."

Once you have approval from the customer's executives to move forward with your deal, and you've gone around to build a coalition of stakeholders within the company, you will have completed a crucial sprint on your Mega Deal journey. But how, exactly, do you *close* a Mega Deal? If you've played your cards right and sewn that red thread of distinctive value all the way through the sales process, closing is straightforward in principle but hard in practice. When everyone from the executives to the people on the ground understands the value you're offering and has bought in, you'd think your Mega Deal could almost close itself.

Well, it might if not for procurement.

CHAPTER SUMMARY

Internal Stakeholder Buy-In: You will need buy-in from your own executives and team members to bring in a whale-sized deal. Use the potential size and strategic importance of the deal as leverage to justify getting A-players on your deal team and non-standard terms for the deal.

Customer Stakeholder Buy-In: Getting broad-based support among customer stakeholders for your deal is like an election campaign. Be paranoid in your Mega Deal sales cycle and stay on the lookout for stakeholders whose approval you don't know you need yet. Beyond one-on-one and group meetings, Preferred Customer Programs and trips to your headquarters are creative ways of differentiating your solution and your company from competition and winning the deal.

Managing Your Team: Mega Deal teams are bigger than typical sales cycle deal teams. They will include one or more executives from your company as well as several A-players across Presales, Product Strategy, Services, etc. Managing a large team through multiple workstreams simultaneously requires sellers to develop skills that look more like project management than sales.

CHAPTER 6

THE FINAL SHOWDOWN WITH PROCUREMENT

I took a deep breath as I dialed into Enginex's conference bridge and steadied myself for the last conference call of the deal I'd spent the past nine months working on. It was the night before the last day of our fiscal year. During the next thirty minutes, I would either close the deal or I wouldn't. There was no more time to make additional changes to the contracts now. This was it.

I was working in my toddler's nursery, sitting on a chair I'd dragged in from the kitchen table. The late-night call was scheduled because the Enginex team was still demanding material changes to the contract, right up to the day before our mutually agreed deadline for signatures. Earlier that morning Bill had called Lars and they agreed a final call was needed to see if the deal could be salvaged.

In the bedroom next door, my wife and son were fast asleep. There was no desk in the nursery, so I'd cleared off the changing table and placed my laptop, phone, and papers on top.

This was going to be an interesting call.

The good news was that I had the right people on the line: Lars, Gunther, and their procurement VP, Stephanie Biers. I felt Lars was on board after our second meeting. We'd also moved the needle with Gunther during our trip to Executive Disneyland, but he still hadn't committed to supporting the deal. I'd spent the last three weeks dividing my time between planning the Disneyland trip and working with Stephanie's team at Enginex on final changes to the contract. The past two weeks had been a blur of activity. We'd gone from 157 negotiation points down to just three, which had already been verbally agreed. The entire contract had been painstakingly laid out, each point hashed and rehashed. Lawyers on both sides of the table had been through it dozens of times. On paper, it was done. Or so we thought.

But Stephanie was the wild card. I didn't know if our negotiations had satisfied her to the point where she would be ready to sign in the next few hours. The compelling event to get this deal done was the end of *our* fiscal year. That meant all the discounts we'd offered were contingent on finalizing the deal in the next twenty-six hours. But it was clear Stephanie had been through dozens, if not hundreds, of similar negotiations. She was a pro. I worried she wouldn't hesitate to extend negotiations past our due date if she wasn't satisfied.

You can do this, I told myself, trying to pump myself up.

There was an eerie sequence of beeps as I authenticated into the secure conference line. Then a prerecorded female voice came over the phone, "You are now joining the conference."

"Jamal Reimer here," I said.

"Hi, Jamal," came an echoey response. "This is Stephanie, and the rest of the team is here as well."

I knew that voice well. Stephanie was the best negotiator I'd ever encountered. She was sharp as a tack and displayed no emotion, and I'd spent so much time talking with her during the past two weeks, I was hearing her voice in my dreams. Actually, I hadn't been getting much sleep. I was on an insane schedule, doing everything in my power to tip this deal into the Closed column.

"We've taken another look at the pricing," Stephanie said, coldly, "and we see the fee for change orders is too high. We need you to reduce it by 35 percent." She stopped talking. *What?* I wanted to scream. *We went over pricing a hundred times and the change order fee never came up as an issue!*

I did a few numbers in my head and realized Stephanie was talking about shaving millions of dollars from the contract. Did she think I'd be able to accommodate that? Throwing a request like this at me so late in the process made things difficult. There wasn't time to get anything else approved by my executives.

"I understand it seems like a high budget for change orders," I said, frantically trying to think of a solution, "but we've been working out this contract for weeks and this is the first time you've mentioned it. The numbers in the contract are based on a careful analysis of your past, current, and predicted future behavior. Unfortunately, I'm not authorized to make any changes to the contract without a legal review and executive approval." I sighed.

"Is that the only point you have?" I asked. "If we can find a way to work that out, are you ready to move forward today?"

"There are two other things," she said. "First, I want to shrink the reporting window so we are notified of mistakes and errors within twelve hours, rather than twenty-four. Also, we'd like access to your SOP documentation so we can more easily check that the work is being done per your standard processes."

"All right," I said, trying to remain calm. "And those three points. Are those the final three things? If we can reach agreement on those points right now on this call, will you be ready to move forward with the deal?"

"Yes," she said.

"OK," I said. "Can you hold for a few minutes so I can bring my management on the line and see what we can get approved right now?"

"Yes," she said. "Please make it quick, as it's quite late here."

I dialed Giovanni, but I wasn't optimistic. Giovanni and Arun were in France at the headquarters of a different customer, negotiating another end-of-year contract. I called both of them, twice, but neither picked up.

Dammit.

The deal I'd had in the bag was disappearing before my eyes. I kicked myself for letting things get so close to the deadline. *If only we had more time*, I thought. But the clock was ticking. I had to get back to Stephanie with an answer. She was growing more impatient with every passing second.

There was nothing I could do. I was in a stalemate. She was asking for things I didn't have the authority to approve, and she was doing it at the last possible minute. Giovanni and Arun were tied up. Any changes to the contract would require their approval as well as input from other teams, which would take days. Bill and Sian couldn't help me. Lars and Andre weren't going to get involved at this point. My deal was toast.

I sighed, closed my eyes, and rubbed my temples, trying to calm down the thumping of my heart. I knew I could wait and push the deal through during the next few weeks. But everything would have to be renegotiated because the current offer was set to expire at the end of the fiscal year. Also, I wouldn't make nearly as much commission if the deal got bumped because the contract would be "on the books" prior to the start of the year and it would be rolled into my new target.

After working around the clock on this deal for nine months, I'd reached the end of the line. Normally I would have some executives on this kind of call with me, but the late timing of the call had made that difficult. I was on my own. I had no choice but to tell Stephanie I couldn't accommodate her request. I had to surrender control and leave the fate of the deal in her hands. There was no telling what she might do.

She had a killer poker face.

Then I remembered someone else with a great poker face: Victor. When I last saw our company's top-secret negotiation master, he'd told me to call him anytime I needed help with this deal. Why didn't I think of that sooner! I punched his number and prayed he'd pick up. The phone rang.

"Victor Boliche," he boomed.

"Victor, it's Jamal," I said, speaking quickly. "I'm on the other line with Enginex. Their procurement VP is making last-minute requests I can't authorize. This call is our last shot to close the deal this fiscal. Giovanni and Arun are negotiating a different deal and I'm on my own."

"I see," Victor said, thoughtful. "Well . . ." I could hear him shift in his seat. "Tell me exactly what she is asking for. Let's get this done right now."

Hope washed over me. I instantly knew I'd made the right decision calling Victor. If anyone could help me close this deal, it was him. I quickly explained the three requests Stephanie was making, and Victor listened intently.

"Our standard operating procedure docs are proprietary," he said, "and altering the pricing for change orders is a god-awful mess and requires a small army to approve. But I think we can work with the reporting window to give her a win here. Let me call upstairs and see if I can get that approved, then I'll join the conference call and work out those points with her."

"That would be awesome, Victor," I said. "Thanks a million."

I hung up and switched back to the conference line where Enginex was waiting.

"Hello, Stephanie," I said, "thanks for your patience. Good news: I was able to get ahold of one of our most senior legal folks. I've told him about your three requests, and he's currently with our corporate approvals department to see what we can do to accommodate you."

"OK, great," she said. "Thanks."

For a tense moment no one spoke. I tried to imagine what Victor was going to say and how Stephanie might respond. Would she really blow up the possibility of getting this deal done over these points? I couldn't get a read on her. One thing I knew is the deal had a lot of support within Enginex. Her superiors were excited about it and wouldn't be happy if she let it slip away.

But was that enough?

A ding shattered the silence, and then Victor Boliche announced himself in that Zeus-like voice.

"Hello, Victor, this is Stephanie Biers," she said. "I'm the lead procurement officer assigned to this deal."

"Hi, Stephanie," Victor replied. "I'm in-house counsel, and Jamal asked me to join the call and see if I could help out."

"Thank you for making yourself available to assist us with this," Stephanie said. "We're just trying to finalize three last points. First, the budget for change orders needs to be reduced by 35 percent. Second, the reporting window should be shrunk to twelve hours, rather than twenty-four. Finally, we'd like access to your SOP docs. We need these changes to move forward."

Wow, Stephanie was good at this. She was stone-cold. I had no idea which points were most important to her, why she was asking for these things, or if she even cared about them at all. Maybe this entire thing was just a power play to see whether we could be pushed around.

Thanks to Victor, I didn't have to figure it out on my own. I felt like the coach who, with thirty seconds left on the clock, calls a time-out and brings his secret weapon into the game—a star player who specializes in just this type of situation. Victor was in position, and I had the feeling I was about to witness a master class in last-minute brinksmanship.

"Firstly," Victor began, "the change request budget is based upon the trend in change requests logged by your operational department over the past several years since we started working together. The trends were discussed and agreed to in the meeting I attended with Lars. The current number was discussed with your team last week and Enginex raised no objections then. It doesn't make sense to revisit now, especially since we've run out of time for pricing reapprovals. Please remember that the whole pricing structure for this deal is contingent on getting a signature by noon tomorrow, so if we hang on this point then the other discounts we've given you will all go away as well."

Victor continued without skipping a beat.

"On the second point, reducing the reporting window isn't something we normally are able to do because we generally have teams working overseas who need that time. However, in this case, I just received special approval from our corporate office to allow a reduction to sixteen hours, provided we stipulate an exception for holidays. Finally, our SOPs are proprietary and are considered a trade secret. Contractually we are on the hook for our deliverables, not to a specific process on how we achieve them. However, I've received another approval for us to affirm in writing that any changes to our SOPs, which happen every couple of years, will not negatively impact the level of service we deliver. This has been approved for Enginex only, and I've been given authority to personally make these changes to your contract tonight."

After a pause, Stephanie spoke. "Thank you," she said, contemplatively. I couldn't tell if she was excited to have gotten some of what she wanted or disappointed that we hadn't given her everything she asked for. "Very well. We can accept a reduction of just 15 percent for the change requests, rather than 35 percent. However, I can't go lower than that, I'm afraid."

The showdown was on. These two expert negotiators were throwing ultimatums at each other, testing for vulnerabilities. She was pushing for every inch she could get. But what could Victor say to talk her down from her position and close the deal without reducing the price tag? Stephanie seemed intent on bringing the cost down.

"Unfortunately, Stephanie," Victor spoke with calm, confident gravitas, "we've run out of time for pricing negotiations. Our services division handles pricing change requests, and any changes would have to be audited by our risk team as well as legal and corporate, all of which are now closed for the night. This is simply being raised too late. If you don't like the terms of the contract as it is written, including the two changes I've already granted, we can renegotiate an entirely new engagement starting next week, once the new fiscal year begins. As you know, our pricing is increasing next year across the board and we are phasing out some elements of your contract that we grandfathered into the current offer as a special favor. Therefore, the deal as it stands today will no longer be available. Either way is fine with us, just let me know how you want to proceed."

Either way is fine with us? I thought. *No it isn't! I need a YES!* I stood up and ran a hand through my hair. My scalp was wet with perspiration. There was a long, uncomfortable pause on the phone, and I paced back and forth along the creaking wood floor, trying not to step on any toys in the dim light.

Adrenaline pumped through my body. Victor had laid everything out in the fair and concise way that only a high-ranking executive could. He'd thrown down the gauntlet, but he did it in the most professional manner possible. He spoke with conviction but without a trace of arrogance or malice. I sat on the edge of my seat, wondering what Stephanie would say next.

It felt like taking a half-court shot in the championship game as the clock hits 0:00.

Over the line came the sound of chairs moving and faint whispering. Then Stephanie came back to the speakerphone, "Well, in that case"— she cleared her throat—"thank you for your time tonight. Send us the final docs with those two changes and we'll have them signed by Lars and Andre before noon tomorrow."

I was incredulous. The deal had reached final agreement, and the price was intact. Victor thanked Stephanie for concluding the negotiations, committed to getting the documents finalized within three hours, and ended the call.

For a good ten seconds, I danced around the darkened nursery like a fool, pumping my arms silently. We were victorious. Almost.

"Victor, you're *amazing!*" I blurted into the phone a moment later.

"I can't believe it!"

"OK, OK," Victor said with a chuckle. "We're not out of the woods yet. I need to get the contract updated and you need to get the dang thing signed before noon tomorrow if Vlad is going to have any chance of getting it booked by midnight. Give me thirty minutes and I'll have the new doc to you."

*   *   *

In the final moments of the Enginex negotiations, all the work I'd done to prove the deal's value and obtain buy-in came into play. The timeline I'd so carefully built, with the compelling event just twenty-six hours away, allowed us to take a hard stance on pricing. I'll never know exactly what was whispered in that room to make Stephanie finally accept our price, but I'm sure it had to do with the fact that Andre, Lars, and Gunther all supported the deal. With so much momentum behind me, even Stephanie couldn't stop the deal from going through.

Defending Your Mega Deal Size

Deal size matters.

It should matter to you personally as a seller because you will deserve an outsize commission check for the over-the-top effort it will take to bring in a Mega Deal. But the real significance of pushing for a high price is that Mega Deals provide your company with significant capital to reinvest in enhancing your offering, hiring for growth, and having greater impact on your customers.

Then there is what I call the Giovanni argument.

When we were close to the end of the pricing negotiations with Enginex, we reached a point where we had covered 97 percent of the pricing components and the size of the deal had just crossed the $50 million mark. I said to Giovanni, "The customer just agreed to $50 *million. Stop* negotiating and let's send them the contract!"

Giovanni looked at me and said, "Jamal, we have an obligation to our company to deliver fair compensation for the value we bring every customer. We are *not* finished yet. I will not stop until we have done our absolute best to negotiate every single point, and neither will you. We owe that to our company. That is why we are here."

His words struck me then and they still do today.

Even after developing a Mega Deal Premise, conducting a successful PoC, and gaining buy-in from all major customer stakeholders, you're still going to have to defend your deal against procurement before it's signed. Every company that's large enough to do a Mega Deal will have a process for vetting suppliers and negotiating deals. This means your deal, sooner or later, is headed for procurement, and you'll have to make it through the final showdown without a significant drop in price before you can call yourself a Mega Dealer.

The procurement team has one job: get the right solutions from the right suppliers at the right price. Once you are selected as the right supplier with the right solution, the experience of working with procurement then becomes "The right price is the lowest price." Procurement may have seen that your price is an order of magnitude higher than that of the competition, but your solution is so compelling, it is chosen regardless. Even at that point, they will work extra hard to get the best deal they can by significantly reducing whatever price you have offered to the business stakeholders. Worse, if they are allowed to independently drive the process, they may try to scrap the deal if they don't get the price they want.

Standard operating procedure for procurement departments is to send the contract out for a Request for Proposal (RFP). If they get competing bids from other vendors, they'll move to create a reverse bidding war, driving the price down until your margins evaporate. Soon the deal you spent months on—developing, championing through multiple levels of the corporate hierarchy, conducting a careful analysis for, and investing hundreds of hours and thousands of dollars in company resources in—is turning into a crapshoot.

Watching a deal disintegrate in your hands is one of the lowest feelings in the world.

You don't want that to happen. I don't want that to happen to you either. I want you to defend 100 percent of the value you're bringing to the table because your company should be fairly compensated for what you deliver. More importantly, the process of proposing and closing such a complex transaction is a ton of work for you as the salesperson, and you deserve to bring in a Mega Deal.

The Infinite Units Dilemma

Products whose value is based on intellectual property are a double-edged sword. In theory, if you're in software or technology or media, it's fantastic to create an asset that can be sold infinitely without being diminished. You write some code or produce a movie once, and then you charge for it as many times as you want. The sky's the limit. There are infinite units available. It's a great business model. But there is a flip side, which I call the Infinite Units Dilemma.

When you're selling a physical product, like eggs, there's a natural limit to how much you can discount your prices and still turn a profit. People understand you can't sell eggs for one cent because the chickens have to be housed and fed and the eggs need to be transported to the store. Similarly, if you're selling hours of people's time, it can be marked down, but not *infinitely*. There's a price floor that the merchant can't drop below and still turn a profit. But with products that have an infinite number of available units, this price floor is not obvious. Once the invention or creation of the IP is paid for, your company can go as low as you want on price. And the procurement people are aware of this. When you have infinite units to sell, your deal value is vulnerable to attack.

Before you can close your Mega Deal, you will come up against a procurement team, whose job is to negotiate price. Let's say your software's list price is $100 per seat and a customer wants ten thousand seats. Procurement might offer you $150,000 and tell you they have offers from three other providers to match that rate. But that price would be an 85 percent discount from your list price. The procurement person will say, "Hey, this is the market price, and it's not like it costs you more to make software just for us, so that's where you'll have to quote to get our business." In other words, they'll use the Infinite Units Dilemma against you. And they're good at it.

The Infinite Units Dilemma is just one example of a weak point that procurement will exploit to drive down the price of your contract. Another strategy procurement uses is commoditization. They will tell you they found multiple other solutions in the market that have the same or similar features as yours and thus position your solution as a commodity. Commodity solutions have commodity pricing. Think a bag of sugar. Not exactly Mega Deal material.

Deconstruction is a tactic where procurement will try to break your proposal into component parts to compare those components with others in the market. This focuses on the *cost* of each part, not the *value* delivered by the whole solution.

Isolation is a fourth tool procurement likes to use against dealmakers.

They will tell everyone at their company to stop communicating with you until the deal is closed. You'll be completely iced out. Without open lines of communication, your visibility into the status of your deal during the decision-making process will be foggy at best. You will not know where you stand and will be more apt to give more to close the deal.

These tactics, and others, are potential weaknesses that procurement will take advantage of.

You need to have some defense mechanisms in place to prevent them. Establishing and defending an uncommonly large deal size is vital in bringing home a Mega Deal. Far and away the most successful strategy to defend against anything procurement throws at you is to have a strong working relationship with senior business stakeholders. By now it may sound like I repeat this refrain too often, but it is so central to Mega Deal construction that its importance manifests in every stage of the sales cycle.

The larger the customer organization you are dealing with, the greater this reality becomes. Business units have mandates. The larger the business unit, the more policies, procedures, and rules are established to control and motivate behavior toward the mandate. Rigidity sets in. In the case of a large procurement group at a large enterprise, they will act toward their mandate of purchasing within their box of guidelines while we as Mega Dealers are working to help the business stakeholders think outside the box to get massive results by adopting our solution. Strong alignment with senior business stakeholders who have bought into the uniqueness and power of your solution is the greatest counterweight to the downward price pressure exerted by procurement.

There are many ways to justify and defend high-deal price tags, and I've used just about all of them. But three strategies in particular work well for a broad spectrum of Mega Deals:

1. **Value:** Underscore the outcome-based benefits of the deal for the customer, like when we showed Enginex how our solution would reduce their risk and save them money.
2. **Volume:** A price argument based on a purchase of many units—users, servers, requests, resource hours, megabytes of data, etc.
3. **Variety:** Bundling different but related products and services together and pricing each one separately.

Here's how the Mega Deal defense strategies work.

1. VALUE

Value is a measure of something's worth, usefulness, or benefit. Value can be positive or negative. In the world of Mega Deals, you can provide value by enabling your customer to avert an impending disaster or empowering them to catapult past a competitor. It's acceptable to frame your deal in terms of either positive or negative value as long as you target the most extreme value possible. This can't be a marginal improvement. Your Mega Deal opportunity can't be a chance to avoid a small amount of pain. It's got to be massive. Your deal needs to represent a transformation, unattainable without significant investment. It's about making competitors obsolete or making the customer's company unique. The value has to be extreme in order to get past procurement at a high price.

Use the results of your PoC to quantify exactly how much your service would be worth to the customer. On the Enginex account, for instance, we built a value argument to justify the high price of our new contract. Previously, the company had been using our pooled offshore resources and sharing access to our analysts with other companies. We created a new option to use a local team. Obviously the locals were more expensive.

But we determined that Lars and Gunther weren't fixated on price. That was a secondary issue. What was costing them the most was risk exposure. So we came up with a value-based argument, centered around reducing the risk of missing critical deadlines. We offered to create a special, dedicated team that would only be used by Enginex. On average, the cost per hour went from $100 to $250, more than doubling the services costs for the contract. But the immense value of reducing the risk that Enginex might miss a deadline was worth millions. We calculated the risk of a missed deadline would drop 78 percent. Despite the five-fold increase in cost, there was enough value to interest them in the deal.

2. VOLUME

The second way to defend the price of a Mega Deal is a volume metric. This is based on the number of transactions, units, projects, files, or data points a customer uses. It works well for contract renewals, where a customer has been using your offering for months or years and you can look back at the data to tease out trends in their usage. Scour the data to find a consistent upward trend with a spike predicted in the not-too-distant future. We didn't attempt this with Enginex because our data showed their usage was consistent and there was no indication of a spike during the next contract cycle. However, imagine how this might play out at a company that provides cloud-based data storage.

Consider two possible scenarios for a customer who is up for renewal soon:

> **Scenario 1:** Their data needs show a steady, gentle upward slope in usage.

> **Scenario 2:** Their data needs are predicted to increase radically next year.

VOLUME METRIC SAMPLE

Both of the graphs seen below show growing internal costs.
Which one provides a stronger emotional reaction?

Scenario 1

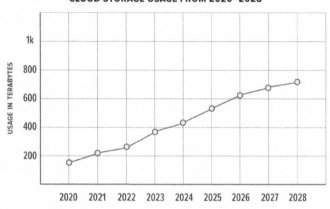

Scenario 2

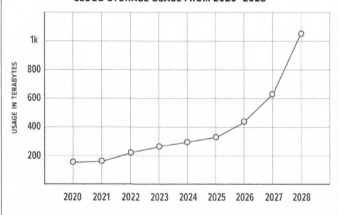

Both graphs show growing storage needs. But Scenario 2, in which costs begin to spike, provokes a stronger emotional reaction in those accountable for those costs.

Steady, predictable trends point to a higher degree of certainty and invoke a sense of calm—even if the trend is in the wrong direction. Uncertainty or volatility grabs attention and provokes anxiety. Our brains are hardwired to fear the unknown. The first and most impactful filter in the brain is the crocodile brain, which assesses information in terms of questions of survival. It has three responses to any situation: should I eat it, should I mate with it, or should I fight or run from it?

Painting a credible picture of an unknown and potentially threatening future to a businessperson awakes a sense of threat and activates the croc brain. In this state, the audience is much more likely to take action to avoid or mitigate the threat. Finding and highlighting data that shows erratic or unpredictable business outcomes can help prepare your audience to make a change to their current way of doing business and facilitate a deal.

3. VARIETY

The final strategy to defend Mega Deal pricing is variety. This is about creating bundled packages with multiple components. Consider how fast-food restaurants ask, "Fries and a soda for just a dollar more?" They're offering you a chance to bundle and save. In enterprise sales, we don't have meal deals; we have the Suite and the Stack.

The Suite works well when you have multiple products that are complementary. If the customer is in pain and your software can provide relief, you'll inform them that, luckily, you've got tools for every piece of the process. First, they need a data collection tool, which is going to suck in and aggregate all the data. Next, a data processing tool is critical. That's going to clean the data and automatically transform it into a usable format. Finally, they are ready for the data analytics tool, which will provide an executive dashboard that pinpoints exactly where their problems are and suggests potential solutions. The customer needs all three tools in order to get a big bang for their buck. That's the Suite.

Compare that to the Stack. Your company might be more of a one-trick pony with a single great product rather than a set of three. In this case, you can bundle the product with add-on components or services to amplify its value for the customer. For example, you could offer implementation services to get it up and running. You could sell ongoing management services as a subscription plan. You might also have training and an annual support conference. Or even a certification program for users to become experts in your product. This is considered a Stack approach because it's centered around a single product and it's bundled with services to complement the product, rather than being grouped with additional products.

Those are the two main ways you can package multiple components of your offer to grow the size of your deal and maintain a high price when you get thrown to the customer's procurement department. Depending on the products and services available at your company, you can get creative with ways to bundle your offerings.

On Enginex, I used a Stack because our contract included not only a license for our software but also a dedicated team of analysts, use of our supercomputer, and custom implementation and integration with their existing systems. This meant their procurement team couldn't attack the overall price of the deal directly. Rather, they had to attempt to bargain down each piece of the contract separately. Even Stephanie's hard-nosed tactics at the end were targeted at just one element of the price, not the entire contract.

When Stakeholder Buy-In Pays Off

One hard thing about doing battle with procurement is that it feels like starting over. They try to cut off access to your previous contacts and are often successful. This is why developing stakeholder buy-in *before* you go to procurement is so critical. If you've done this right, you'll now have access to a number of chess pieces on *their* side of the board. They can't box you in because you've got players all over the place who are senior enough to rebuff procurement's calls for channeling all communications through them.

When you've practiced the art of Executive Whispering well, it's nearly impossible for procurement to stop an ongoing dialogue between two Senior Vice Presidents. Having friends in high places makes it harder for them to treat you like a commodity.

But that doesn't mean they won't try.

Mark Coombs, the Mega Dealer whose AI patent review product we saw back in Chapter One, had another big deal that got stuck in procurement. So he scheduled a meeting with his lead contact at the customer's company, an EVP, and brought his CEO and main SVP supporter with him. They did a whiteboard session mapping out pain points all over the EVP's kingdom. Finally the EVP said, "Well, it's clear we need this." Then he turned to the VP sitting next to him and said, "John, where is the deal right now?"

"Well," said John, a little sheepishly, "it's currently stuck with Steve in procurement. He's been going back and forth on the contract for a couple months now."

The EVP thought for a moment.

Then he said, "OK, take Steve off the project. We need someone who is a more strategic thinker. Just wrap up the deal and get it done."

"Yes, sir," John said. "I'll round up everyone and get it pushed through."

True story.

I've seen variations of this play out on other deals too. When you play your cards right with the customer's senior management, you can get your deal fast-tracked through procurement and greatly simplify the negotiation process. However, you're still going to need to prepare for at least some negotiation. Nobody wants to sign a multimillion-dollar deal without making sure it offers the best possible terms they can get. Negotiation is necessary.

Let's be clear. Despite what procurement may say about their holistic approach to working with suppliers, when it comes time to negotiate the deal, their focus is *price*. To balance that, your job is to focus on *value*. Procurement will add complexity by creating comparisons with several competitive offerings to reduce your uniqueness and commoditize your solution.

One tactic you can use is to craft a simple yet profound statement that sums up your entire message, known as a Knockout Punch. Shorter than an elevator pitch, a Knockout Punch is something you should be able to deliver in a single sentence. Practice it until you can say it with charisma.

Because it is so simple and easy to remember, a Knockout Punch evokes a strong mental image of extreme value. Wrapped up in this little package, any customer stakeholder you deliver it to will be able to take it around and share it with colleagues during their internal discussions. Knockout Punches help your supporters sell your value and uniqueness in a way that will stick and spread. Once you've propagated a Knockout Punch through an account, procurement will be playing a losing game of whack-a-mole trying to counter it.

Frame your Knockout Punch by expressing the value of your solution in a ratio of either 3-to-1, 5-to-1, or 10-to-1. Show that things got three, five, or ten times better in some way for the customer after implementing your solution during the PoC.

For example, I once created a Knockout Punch called "Legos, not trains." The idea was that most enterprises needed many software applications to manage their business processes and those applications needed to be hand-sewn together with custom integrations. I explained this concept to my four-year-old while we were playing one day by connecting two wooden train cars with a blob of Play-Doh. Not a very elegant solution, but very common in the market.

However, Legos are specifically made so they can just snap together. And they stay attached forever until you take them apart. I made stacks of connected pieces and fitted them onto the flat Lego base we used to make Lego castles. My mother-in-law, watching the whole thing from the playroom doorway, got the analogy instantly. Legos—that's the one-word analogy for my company's preintegrated solution, in which microservices don't need integration because everything natively plays well together.

Long before I encountered procurement, I set up the idea of Legos versus trains at the start of my presentation. Then I went through my whole pitch, and at the end I came back for the Knockout Punch: "Remember, guys, what you want is Legos, not trains. That's a ten-to-one improvement. Legos, not trains."

Knock. Out. Punch.

I learned the customer's people were talking about that line for weeks afterward, selling the concept to each other and doing my job for me. The strong visual combined with the simple ratio was so easy to understand that it disseminated rapidly, growing my sphere of influence within the company. After that, the reference was a lever to pull in any conversation to bring to mind the 10x value proposition I was bringing to the table.

Bob Iger also used a Knockout Punch to close the deal with his board to buy Pixar. Multiple times over the course of a few months, he repeated the phrase "As Disney Animation goes, so goes the company," emphasizing the need to fix Disney's animated-film problem above all other priorities. This was also one of the last lines he uttered before the board voted on whether or not to support the deal. It was his Knockout Punch.

Build your own Knockout Punch using a very basic analogy and a simple but powerful ratio. This single tagline will give you unparalleled leverage. Procurement will have their work cut out for them to stop you from closing on your terms.

Are You Willing to Walk Away?

Another factor that can seriously accelerate the Mega Deal cycle is a willingness to leave the table. Neediness and desperation do nothing but give procurement leverage against you. When customers sense a contract is more important to you than to them, they'll purposely drag their feet to wait for better terms. Or they might request contract changes late in the game when you're up against a tight deadline, like Stephanie did during the Enginex negotiations.

Complicating this further is the fact that it's hard to walk away from an opportunity after your sales team, development team, management team, and executive team have all put time and effort into a long sales cycle. At this point you're invested, and your customer's procurement team knows it.

There are many subtleties involved in letting your customer know you're willing to walk away from a major deal, and I've made some big mistakes. The major reason to walk away from a deal is a lack of serious engagement. If it seems like the person is toying with you, get out. Even a customer who is mad at you is better than one who doesn't care. An angry or frustrated customer *wants something* and will engage with you, even if they yell at you when you get them on the phone. But an apathetic customer will just ignore your calls and leave your emails unread. If this is happening to you, sometimes walking away can cause the customer to realize you are not desperate, and they will reengage.

I know one sales writer, John Holland of Customer Centric Selling, who has a great approach for tempting a customer to reengage with a dead offer. He calls it the Take Back Letter. When someone you've been communicating with suddenly stops responding after you sent an offer, John recommends writing a formal letter rescinding the offer. Tell the customer that, since you've tried to follow up numerous times and haven't heard anything back, you are canceling the offer and it is no longer valid. So if they decide to reengage, you will put together a new offer for them. About 40 percent of your dead offers will come back to life when you send one of these letters. Not a bad investment for the price of a postage stamp.

During my third Mega Deal, my team and I almost walked. It came down to the wire. My VP of Sales and I agreed we were at our walk-away number, the price below which it did not make sense to do the deal. We decided we would not go any further, and then the customer's procurement guy said, "If that's the case, we probably don't have a deal." So my VP went for the final gambit. He said, "Take that back to your management. If they agree we don't have a deal, then we'll pack it up."

Two days later we got the deal.

One of the most important things about walking away from a deal is you have to know your walk-away number. You should know this way in advance, before the emotional phase of the negotiations kicks in and you start to lose the ability to think rationally. If you try to make a decision about whether to walk while you're in the middle of negotiations, your sense of ownership will drag you into negative territory—either through discounting too much or agreeing to unacceptable terms—turning your Mega Deal into a Mega Zombie. So decide before you sit down with procurement where your limits are.

Toward the end of the journey you might start to feel like a hobbit from *The Lord of the Rings* walking into the volcanic wasteland of Mordor. It may seem you're at the end of the world and there's nothing around you but smoke and lava. Reaching the end of a Mega Deal is nerve-wracking and it sucks. There will be sleepless nights, personal sacrifices of time and attention to loved ones, and a constant pressure to get the deal done. Your whole team and chain of command will be watching and pinging you endlessly for updates. The situation will call on you to perform beyond what you thought you were capable of. But if you do endure, if you press on, you will be crowned. And once crowned, you will no longer be a sales rep.

You will be a Mega Dealer.

The Last Day

Victor sent me the revised contracts, then I converted them to PDFs and emailed them over to Stephanie and the project team. The following morning, at 7:15 a.m., I sent off an email to Lars and Andre, letting them know we'd reached verbal agreement on all points with procurement, and the contracts had been shipped with the expectation that signatures would be delivered before noon. With the short timeline on this deal, I wanted to make sure there was pressure on Stephanie from above.

Then there was nothing to do but wait.

7:24 a.m.: I made coffee and breakfast. The eggs were taking forever to cook. Was the stove on? Yes. I was just anxious. Time couldn't move fast enough. By noon the waiting would be over. We would either have the signed contracts or we wouldn't.

8:31 a.m.: I checked my emails. Again. Nothing yet. I couldn't work because I couldn't concentrate. All I could think about was Enginex. So I tidied the apartment. After some dusting and scrubbing, taking stacks of old papers out for recycling, and going through my drawers, I checked my email again. Still nothing.

9:04 a.m.: I tried meditating, but it was useless. After sitting and breathing for what felt like half an hour, I opened my eyes to check the time and found only three minutes had passed. *Is it just me or is time moving at one-tenth of its regular speed?* I wondered.

By the time I made it into the office, I was a wreck. Every time my phone buzzed, I lunged at it like a cobra, reaching across the desk to devour whatever notification happened to come through.

```
Simon Feltz wants to connect on
LinkedIn

Any thoughts on dinner tonight?

Your credit card on file will
expire soon. Please update your
payment method.

Jasper Gruening liked your post
```

Hey Jamal, we're having an end of
the year lunch, noon at Oscars,
you in?

Netflix recommends these shows
for you

Finally a different kind of notification came through my inbox. It was from our comptroller, and it said a contract had been received in my name. I sat down to steady myself as I pulled up the email. I felt light-headed, and my heart was beating like an Olympic sprinter's after a race.

With shaking hands I opened the email and found a ZIP file attached. I couldn't access it on my phone. *Dang!* I sprinted to my desk and ripped open my laptop. My fingers whizzed across the keys as I logged in. For an agonizing minute, I sat there as my computer slowly booted up, my body tensed. Finally, the desktop came into view, and I was able to open my email and bring up the attachment.

Unzipping . . .

Inside of the file there were eight PDFs, one for each contract involved in this deal. I found the master contract, scrolled to the bottom, and verified that it was, indeed, signed. Yes, there was Lars Reinhoff's messy signature and CFO Andre Veldspar's. Then I scrolled back to the top to check the price again, just to be absolutely sure it was right.

There it was in black and white: $53,000,000.

When I saw that number, I stood up and let out a yell (which startled every office worker within thirty feet of me). The room started spinning, and I had to sit down again to stop myself from passing out. It seemed like a weight had been lifted from my chest, and my ears were ringing.

I shook myself and forwarded the contract to Giovanni, Arun, and the rest of the team, and I cc'd our senior management. I included a detailed email thanking everyone who worked on the deal, along with a comment about how each individual had contributed.

Then I went to meet my family for a late lunch at a café down on the bay. We sat on the patio as the afternoon sun cast a warm orange glow over the windswept harbor. I was still shell-shocked by the abrupt finality of the moment. My ears were ringing and everything felt slower, like I was underwater. The world was a blur. But I felt my wife's hand on my knee, and I took a deep breath, relaxing and trying to let go of the stress of the past few months.

My phone was buzzing nonstop in my pocket. Finally, I took a look at the screen. It was full of messages from people congratulating me on the deal:

> Congrats on closing your deal!
>
> You're a hero and a legend!
>
> You da man, Jamal!
>
> Wow, you did it!
>
> What a great accomplishment!

"Hey, kids," my wife said, beaming, "today was an important day. You know that big project Daddy's been working on, that he's been putting so much effort into?"

They nodded. My kids knew all about Enginex. They knew I hadn't had as much time to play with them lately or talk to them about their lives, because I'd been focused on my "big project." They knew

I was grouchy more often because I was distracted, thinking about the "big deal." They knew I kept telling them "as soon as this deal is over, sweetie."

"Well," my wife continued, breaking into a wide smile, "it's over! Daddy got the deal and now it's done!"

My kids cheered and rushed to tell me what they were most excited to do with me. "I want to play with trucks!" said my son. "Can we have a tea party?" asked my daughter.

I wrapped them up in a hug. But something about the way my wife had said "Daddy got the deal" didn't sit right with me. It was the same message that was coming at me in the texts and emails that were blowing up my phone: "You're a star," "You did it," and "Nice job." Everyone was congratulating me personally and referring to it as "my" deal. But it wasn't my deal at all. It dawned on me that I hadn't independently executed *any* of the key tasks that brought the deal home.

I hadn't even recognized the potential for the Mega Deal; Giovanni had been the one who first pointed out that this contract could be worth $50 million. Nor did I develop the Distinctive Value Proposition on my own; Arun helped me realize that a designated team might solve Enginex's problem. Similarly, it was Bill McClellan's charm, wit, and executive status that got us the first meeting with Lars Reinhoff and sold him on the PoC. Then Giovanni made sense of the data and pitched Lars on the need for a dedicated team. Finally, it was Victor who saved the deal from slipping out of the fiscal year by getting last-minute approvals and calling Stephanie's bluff, and it was Vlad who filed all the paperwork.

How was this considered "my" deal when all of the major pieces had been executed by other people?

It was in that moment that I fully realized how different the last nine months had been from everything I'd done before. Closing a Mega Deal was nothing like the standard sales process. It was a whole different world.

It's not that selling Enginex hadn't been a lot of work. In fact, I'd worked harder on this deal than I'd worked on anything in my life. The past nine months had seen more all-nighters, hundred-hour weeks, and weekends away from my family than any other period of my career. But it was a different kind of work. It wasn't the typical solitary sales pursuit, where the rep sells the customer and closes the deal with minimal assistance. It was a team effort involving the skills and expertise of ten people. I couldn't have done it without my talented and devoted team, and they never would have done it without me either.

I had added value to this deal in completely different ways than usual; for example:

- I engaged my company's executives so I could ask them to deploy resources when I needed them.
- At every roadblock, I brought in people who were best suited to deal with the issue (not me).
- I was the glue that held the team together, the alarm that sounded when things went wrong, and the fixer who found creative ways to solve problems.
- I never gave up, even when things looked unfixable.
- I insisted on finding massive, customer-specific value.

The experience of closing this deal had changed the way I thought about my role and abilities.

Over the coming years, I would close two more deals worth over $50 million each. I would also line up a single deal worth over $100 million, only to lose it. These incredibly impactful deals became familiar, expected. My relationships with my own management team and those of my customers changed. I not only asked them for help and advice now and again, but they reached out to me for the same. My performance carved out a special place for me in my organization. It was my new normal, and I liked it.

I had become a Mega Dealer.

Back at the café, however, I was exhausted. And I hadn't spent quality time with my family in what seemed like an eternity. I sat both my kids down on my lap, one on each knee, and looked them in the eyes. Finally, I relaxed a little. After all, my commission from this deal would more than quadruple my salary. I could afford to take some time off and spend it with my family.

"OK," I said, laughing, "we can do all of that. I'm yours. We can do anything we want."

My kids cheered again, and I broke into a huge dorky grin. For a long time the words echoed in my head: *We can do anything we want.*

With this deal it was finally true.

CHAPTER SUMMARY

Defending Mega Deal Pricing: By nature, Mega Deals receive extra scrutiny from customers, primarily from their procurement team. You need to be prepared to defend your price—procurement will try to significantly reduce it.

Deliver a Knockout Punch: Create a simple but profound phrase or sentence that summarizes the value provided by your offering.

The Problem of Infinite Units: Many IP-based businesses offer solutions with infinite units available (software or movies, for example). The product is created once but can be sold infinitely. This makes establishing value abstract and subjective. Procurement will play that to their advantage.

How to Defend Your Mega Deal Size: Below are strategies that will help make your offering's value more concrete and defendable:

1. **Value:** Elite reps position a Mega Deal's value on a continuum between the concepts of pleasure and pain, two of the most compelling motivators for change. To justify massive investment in a project, the yield must be greater than the investment in areas of high priority for senior management.

2. **Volume:** Defending a Mega Deal's size can come down to an articulation of the sheer volume of units required to achieve the outsize benefit and a convincing justification of the need for so many units. The volume argument almost always comes down to expert interpretation of credible customer-specific data.

3. **Variety:** This is about bundling packages that have multiple components. There are two main ways to structure a bundled offering: the Suite and the Stack.

Be Willing to Walk Away: When negotiations reach your walk-away number or your customer disengages, it might be time to walk away from the deal. Sometimes this can actually revive a dead deal and cause the customer to chase you.

EPILOGUE

LIFE AS A MEGA DEALER

Some things have changed radically in the years since the Enginex deal, while others have stayed largely the same. Giovanni hasn't changed a bit. He's still at the same company, doing huge deals, riding motorcycles, eating fresh oysters, and performing impressive mental math at all hours of the day and night. Currently he's building his fifth home, in the Bahamas.

Victor hasn't changed either. He's still flying around the world negotiating the company's biggest contracts. I talk to him occasionally, but he can only be found when he wants to be.

Arun retired shortly after the Enginex deal. Except he's not *really* retired. Arun just retired from our company (at the age of fifty-eight), and now he's pursuing a PhD in physics and serves on the board of directors for several startups.

Bill was appointed EVP and worldwide head of sales. Outside of his day job, he also runs a mastermind group for startup CEOs. He has shifted his high-end collection interests from exotic cars to large powerboats.

Lars got hired away from Enginex to work for an emerging insurance company, where he now serves as the CFO and is getting ready to take the company public. You can bet I've stayed in close touch with Lars, and we currently have a large deal in the works with his new company.

Gunther was promoted to Lars's old position, and now he's the EVP at Enginex and has become the new executive sponsor for our engagement. Thankfully, my relationship with Gunther has been great ever since our trip to Executive Disneyland. I've come to realize his frowns don't mean he isn't interested, he's just not a smiley person.

The biggest changes of all have been in my own life. After closing the Enginex deal, I was invited to the President's Club, an incentive trip our company hosts once per year for the very top performing salespeople. After four days adventuring and relaxing on the beach with colleagues from around the world, I found myself at the final banquet watching our CEO, Sian Blackstone, standing at the podium to recognize the top sales reps in our global organization.

"I want to tell you about the biggest deal of the year," he said. "We have an account exec here with us today who closed a single contract worth $53 million."

When I heard that number, I got chills. He was talking about my deal. My hands and feet went numb, and my throat suddenly felt dry. A bead of sweat was forming on my cheek.

"This rep was kicked off the account a couple years ago when a new management team came in as part of an acquisition," Sian continued. "But he got it back this year at a time when the customer was seriously unhappy. It looked like the contract renewal was going to be lost to another provider. Then our rep got the attention of some top customer executives and was able to not just close the deal at $10 million, but expand it to $53 million!"

People cheered. I was listening almost in disbelief, recalling all the impediments that should have derailed the deal along the way. I was amazed we had made it to this moment.

"Ladies and gentlemen," he said, after a small pause, "the award for the biggest deal of the year goes to . . . Jamal Reimer!"

The place went nuts. I turned a bright shade of red from the attention. At the front of the room, Sian was holding up a plaque.

"Come on up here, Jamal," he said.

In the photo a company photographer captured of that moment, I look stunned, grinning and clutching the award as I shake Sian's hand. That night I was on top of the world.

But I kept thinking of all the people who made the deal happen.

So when I got home I made a list of everyone who had gone the extra mile to contribute to the Enginex win, and I placed it on my desk next to my open laptop. Then I went online and bought every one of them a gift. I also did what I could to get the company to max out any potential bonuses they were eligible for. I wanted to show my appreciation for their contributions.

A week later, I got an email from Bill McClellan. He wanted to meet for lunch.

"Let's cut the small talk," he said, as we sat down at Bill's favorite burger bar, a place he loved for their all-you-can-eat fries. "You know why we're here, Jamal," he told me.

Uh, I do? I dunked a fry into some ketchup, hoping Bill would keep talking. I had no idea what to say.

"Do you know we have over forty different reps selling to Enginex across all of our ten thousand products?" he asked. "They buy a lot from us. I think they are big enough to make them a Key Account. And I want to make you the Key Account Director. That means you would be in charge of all the reps who sell to Enginex—over forty people. You would become accountable for our overall relationship with that customer and our sales strategy as a whole. It's a new job that comes with more responsibility, more opportunity, and, of course, a nice raise. What do you say, Jamal?"

Once again, I was stunned speechless. All I could do was nod my head in gratitude.

The biggest surprise for me, however, came when I met with a member of our compensation team to review my commission. That's when I was able to confirm that the Enginex deal had *quadrupled* my total compensation. That was a moment of huge gratitude.

My wife and I decided to sock away 100 percent of my commission on the Enginex deal, a habit I've continued with all of my Mega Deal commissions. This has brought me to the point where I could now retire any time and support my current lifestyle on savings alone.

It's an amazing position to be in.

The Enginex deal set me on a fast track to financial security, and it put me on a rocketing sales career trajectory. Thanks to this deal, I was finally able to work for my own *fulfillment*, not for a paycheck or to boost my ego.

Opportunities beyond work sprang up as well. I was invited to appear on several sales podcasts about uncommonly large deals, and the topic was so popular I had thousands of reps connect with me on LinkedIn. Today, I am focused on empowering others to do Mega Deals of their own. I coach individual reps and teams on how to find and close Mega Deals, and consult with companies on Mega Deal enablement. I write a newsletter for enterprise sellers called *The A-List*. Plus, I'm a VP of Sales for a SaaS company, which keeps me active in the field and pursuing Mega Deals of my own.

There's also been a change in my self-perception. It's not that I wasn't confident before, but I've reached a different level in my mindset. When you do something greater than you ever imagined was possible, there's a mental shift that happens. That accomplishment, which at first seems almost impossible, is no longer a mystery.

It's knowable and doable. Because you *did* it.

Every Mega Deal you close will be momentous and impactful, but none will be as profound as your first—it changes you. Your tenth Mega Deal takes you from nine to ten, but your first takes you from zero to one. That changes everything. Legendary venture capitalist Peter Thiel wrote an entire book about this concept, called *Zero to One*. Doing things that have never been done before is the best way to profit economically and move the human race forward, Thiel says. That's the embodiment of the Mega Deal mindset. That's what gets the biggest dealmakers out of bed every day: doing something that has never been done.

Even though the experience of closing the Enginex deal was mentally, emotionally, and physically exhausting, it left me feeling more energized and excited than ever. I'd made an impact. After attending the President's Club trip and recovering with my family for a couple of weeks, I was ready to return to work and tackle my next Mega Deal. In fact, after my experience with Enginex, it was hard to imagine ever returning to the Land of Run-Rate Selling. There was no way I could go back to the grind I'd been living before. I'd gotten a taste of the world of the Mega Dealer, and I was hungry for more. As far as I saw it, the benefits far outweighed the pain.

Before I learned how to find and close Mega Deals, I existed in a world of scarcity, fear, and mind-numbing repetition: the Land of Run-Rate Selling. I always felt I had the worst territory on the team. I would chase every small opportunity like a squirrel socking away nuts for the winter. I constantly feared underperforming and all the undesirable consequences that came with it. Out of a lack of knowing what else to do, I would resort to increased cold outreach with the goal of getting any activity going. Even during good quarters, when I made my number, I was just moving product. There was no sense of contributing to the greater good.

After the Enginex deal, I looked back on that world and vowed never to return to it. I made a short list of what I wanted to give and receive from my practice of enterprise sales:

- **Be prosperous:** I want to be able to generate superior earnings to afford myself financial freedom, to provide well for my family, and to give myself the ability to retire early.
- **Make a difference:** I believe the purpose of life is to contribute more than to receive, to serve more than to be served. I want to have a positive impact on the lives of as many people as possible by executing my profession in the spirit of service.
- **Grow perpetually:** To reach my professional potential I need to practice skills I already know to achieve mastery and continue learning new things to expand my capabilities.

Choose Your Own Trajectory

If you share my dread of the Land of Run-Rate Selling and if you have aspirations like those on my short list above, then I wholeheartedly encourage you to start your journey to become a Mega Dealer. For individual contributors, it is the only space within the enterprise selling world where the highest level of prosperity, impact, and growth are possible. When you master this art, you will rise beyond the turbulence of transactional selling to sell above the clouds. For Mega Dealers, sales becomes a fulfilling and meaningful journey where they spend their days engaged in activities that drive toward massive results. They have a huge impact on their company, their customers, and their customer's customers.

This book is intended to give any enterprise seller an authentic view of what it takes to land a Mega Deal. It also provides you with a road map for your own Mega Deal journey. My Mega Deal story was not a straight line (no large-deal pursuit is) and you may be feeling overwhelmed with all the detail and not sure where to begin.

If I were back at the beginning and starting all over again, here is what I would do:

1. Read the most recent annual report for one to three of your highest priority accounts.
2. Find a credible link between an objective mentioned in the annual report and a capability or benefit your offering can deliver.
3. Socialize the potential value you found with customer stakeholders who are close to decision-makers to see if they find it compelling, and if so, enlist their support for a meaningful deal pursuit.

4. Document everything as you plan and execute your Mega Deal strategy. The free resources at megadealsecrets.com/downloads will help you with tools and templates.

5. Don't just expect to read this book once and close a massive deal. Treat it like a playbook. Go back and review Chapter One while you build your premise around a customer's Core Imperative, a compelling C-Level Insight, and a Distinctive Value Proposition. Your Mega Deal Premise will be the foundation upon which you can build your Mega Deal.

Accelerate Your Mega Deal Journey

Over the past two years, I have worked with ambitious enterprise sellers to help them find and close Mega Deals.

- **Alex** went from selling $40,000 deals to $600,000 deals in six months.
- The average deal size at **Mark**'s company was $90,000. At the time of publication, Mark was on track to close multiple seven-figure deals in the next fiscal year.
- **Gunner** used to close $150,000 deals, and after nine months of working together, he brought in a $3,500,000+ deal that landed him the Rookie of the Year Award at his company.

My own Mega Deal journey involved over a decade of trial and error, along with many false starts and failures. My results did not materially improve until I finally found the right mentors in my twelfth year as an enterprise seller. You could take a similar path and hope you'll get to your destination eventually, or you can accelerate your progress by working with me and my team like the sellers mentioned above, and take the journey with other sellers who are on the same mission as you. If you would like to join my community of Mega Dealers, visit:

megadealsecrets.com

Whatever path you choose on your Mega Deal journey, I encourage you to take your first step today. Set yourself a Big Hairy Audacious Goal to close a Mega Deal during the next year. Write it down and tell people about it. Take the five steps I listed above. Sign up to get my free content at megadealsecrets.com/a-list—take some small actions right away to create momentum. Leaving the Land of Run-Rate Selling and joining the world of Mega Deals is a personal and professional transformation that is absolutely worth taking. I've done my best to paint a picture of what the view is like from atop the Mega Deal mountain. Now it is up to you to figure out your own ascent.

With that, I will leave you with one of my favorite quotes, from novelist John Green: "What is the point of being alive if you don't at least try to do something remarkable?"

Mega Dealers are the crazy people who dare to try.

REVIEW REQUEST

Welcome to the world of Mega Dealers!

I hope you loved this book.

If you did, would you mind leaving a fellow Mega Dealer an honest review on Amazon?

Thank you so much!

ACKNOWLEDGMENTS

Although this book is about my story, there were a host of contributors who made it happen, gave it life and meaning.

I first want to thank my writer, Andy Earle. Although we both spent months banging away at keyboards, Andy's storytelling ability made every chapter an engaging experience that grabs the audience's attention and brings them into every scene.

The characters in the book are real people. My colleagues and customer stakeholders from my first Mega Deal saga each played a role in the story and taught me something new along the way. The real-life personalities behind the book's characters Giovanni Lamere and Arun Baines were truly my Mega Deal mentors, and although their real names will remain anonymous here, they know who they are and I can't thank them enough, as they taught me my craft and, in so doing, changed my life forever.

I was blessed to have had a book team assembled from some of the most creative and ambitious enterprise sellers I have known: Anthony Lopez, Alexander Brockman, Mark Coombs, Paul Turner, Ron Masi, and Andrew Mewborn. Throughout the writing process I would send them every new chapter upon its completion, which they would read and critique on weekly calls that went on for months. It is their perspectives that shaped the telling of the story into a form that would be of the most use to individual contributors everywhere.

There were several sellers whose stories were also incorporated into the book, including Joe Paranteau, Ron Masi, and Mark Coombs. Their real-life stories of closing Mega Deals brought a variety of experiences that adds so much richness to the book by giving multiple perspectives on the topic.

I am indebted to my book production manager, Maria Gagliano of The Pub Pros. She kept the entire project rolling and on track and was an indispensable counselor through the publishing process, without whom I never would have made it to the finish line.

Special thanks go to my illustrator, Lorna Nakell. Lorna not only rendered compelling illustrations, but she challenged me to use imagery, analogies, and supporting text that conveyed the spirit of my points in the most clear and simple ways possible. Her work significantly increased the quality of the book.

Most of all I want to thank my family. My wife, Didar, and children, Silas and Nuria. They bore the brunt of the sacrifice of my time on weekend mornings or weekday evenings for over a year. Thank you for putting up with this project.

Made in the USA
Coppell, TX
12 June 2023

17982639R00142